ALTERNATIVES
for ART EDUCATION
RESEARCH

TRENDS IN ART EDUCATION

Consulting Editor: **Earl Linderman**
Arizona State University

ART FOR EXCEPTIONAL CHILDREN—DONALD UHLIN,
Sacramento State College

Alternatives for ART EDUCATION RESEARCH

Inquiry into the making of art

Kenneth R. Beittel
The Pennsylvania State University

WM. C. BROWN COMPANY PUBLISHERS
Dubuque, Iowa

Copyright © 1973 by Wm. C. Brown Company Publishers

Library of Congress Catalog Card Number: 72—88899

ISBN 0—697—03293—0

Printed in the United States of America

Contents

Preface

For twenty years I have been associated with research in art education, both my own and that of the many doctoral students I have advised. During the first fifteen years of this period, I pursued, and encouraged others to pursue, inquiries based on models from the social sciences where empiricism wedded with logical positivism and public verificationism was the norm. The achievements of a behaviorism or neobehaviorism emulating earlier concepts of natural science are well enough known that I need not detail them here. The deficiencies and inadequately grasped philosophical presuppositions of such approaches are less well known, and it was these that little by little became an overpowering influence toward change in my own research experience.

Without retelling this personal history (for which I can find some impersonal basis in the culture and in the climate of art education as well), suffice it to say that I conceive this transition as symbolizing a return to earlier root metaphors in art education —for example, the transformational parallels between making art and developing a self-system. It is also a return to the experiential core of art, the expressive situation, and the spread of one situation to others. The primary evidence of unique experiential events, when it comes to the making of art, crowds out the pale and indirect means upon which a neopositivistic behaviorism depends for its data. More than that, the latter, while not in error in itself, permits one all too easily to ignore the experiential base without which the very idea of art lacks credulity.

In addition, I believe that the research enterprise has been inflated and wrongly adulated, partly because of a scientific cosmology whose myths have hidden from us the fact that power, control, and economics have been equally as important in our institutional world as the honest pursuit of knowledge. It is no longer possible to remain innocent before the question: To what end this knowledge? This has led to a reflexivity on the researcher's part which I consider necessary and healthy.

Further, I no longer feel we can look to psychology, to philosophy, or to any other discipline for models and methods sufficiently sensitive to our own needs and desires. We must remain interdisciplinary in scope and interest, and we cannot afford to be insular and naive. Nevertheless, I believe that we alone can do research sensitive to those art and life connections which are the basic phenomena of our field and practice.

Relieved of the political pressures and removed from the unscholarly judgments of scholars as to how one "must" do research, however, I feel no need to defend or attack any methods for research. What I am presenting in this volume are alternatives closer to the qualitative, experiential, phenomenological side. It is my hope that these will lead young and old alike to rethink and refeel the meaning of art experience for themselves and others, through bringing us closer to the order and to the chaos of creation and to ourselves as limited minds trying to understand these. Such approaches should be judged on whether they make us more sensitive and responsive practitioners and theorists. In terms of research, they should be weighed as to whether they encourage further inquiry and increase meaningful dialogue in art education.

I admit to my amateur standing in these modes and hope that others will soon go beyond my work in print. The examples are limited to the conditions of my own research and these limits should not be confused with the potential of the modes themselves. In like manner, it is conceivable that others may not wish to operate within the two major assumptions underlying my use of the modes presented. Simply put, I have assumed that to study the making of art one must move as closely as possible (though only by indirect access can this be done) to the creating stream of consciousness; and I have assumed that a special participant observer role is essential to this closeness.

I envision this book being used in art education research seminars, in research units of other classes, and in general seminars and classes dealing with the theory and philosophy of art education. Its purpose is served if it invites exploration, inquiry, and lively discussion.

I wish to acknowledge the many contributions to my thought and its development made by my recent research assistants, particularly Charles S. Steele, Frederick Burkett, Suzanne Merriam, Don J. Stapleton, Barbara White Kazanis, and Vitold Kobicz, as well as by other graduate students and departmental colleagues at Penn State. I owe Earl Linderman, editor of this series, my thanks for his support in encouraging me to make this an honest exploration in research method and not an academic exercise. The Department of Art Education at Penn State has continued to grant me time and space to pursue my research into drawing. During the time I was writing this I was able to receive support through a small contract grant from the U.S. Office of Education, which allowed me to have, formally, one research assistant, Frederick Burkett, and also covered costs of supplies and materials. Finally, my wife, Esther, has given me that long-range support and encouragement which nurtures such projects into being.

1 Introduction, Assumptions and Purposes

This book is an attack on "methodolatry"—that disease of the Western mind which makes an idol of method, separating means from ends, motive from goal, and experiencing from knowing.

Not that the latter antinomies can be ignored or transcended. The tension between them is perpetual and indissoluble. They are part of the human condition, as is the all-too-human desire for resolution toward complete flux on the one hand or complete control on the other. These are pseudo-solutions to our condition which variously appeal to our exuberant youthfulness or cautious maturity, as to an overdrawn art or science.

Dewey has cautioned us against confounding "having an experience" and "knowing," suggesting that these are functional or role differences worth preserving (although here, again, the antinomies explode upon us in a deeper immersion, and we feel as though we know in the midst of experiencing, and we cannot forget that the process called "knowing" is decidedly experiential). Yet Dewey also describes how the "pervasive quality" of a situation, a decidedly experiential phenomenon, integrates and guides the more cognitive process of knowing.[1] I accept this simultaneously unified and differentiated definition of experiencing and knowing as a base for my inquiry into "making art."

There are a number of additional assumptions upon which this work is predicated. One is that art is an "ultimate" realm of human experience[2]— that is, it cannot be reduced to nor assimilated by other likewise essentially autonomous realms, such as religion or science. This does not mean that what are here termed autonomous realms cannot interact and overlap, nor does it contradict the belief that all such realms have at base a common human condition. "Making art" is as basic a possession of man as "language competence."[3] Like the latter, it transcends particular cultures and defies our developmental and psychological analyses to the place where we end up mumbling apologetically of its innateness. Further, as with language, the structures upon which its functioning would seem to depend precede the precise skills and mastery exemplified by its rather sudden and almost full possession.[4]

Thus, a preschool child, in what Lowenfeld termed the preschematic and the scribbling stages,[5] will already give evidence of what I will call artistic causality, idiosyncratic meaning, and intentional symbolization.[6] I take the latter terms to be essential conditions for making art. By "artistic causality" I merely affirm the agency of the artist, the fact that he feels like an "origin" and not a "pawn."[7] The term connotes an active helmsman plotting his course according to his interpretation of in-process feedback. The philosophical conundrum of whether situational acts are predetermined I must by-pass.[8] Suffice it to say that to the artist, even when a work seemingly works its own way through him, he stands at the least in a similar relationship to it as the mother to the child in gestation. Usually this is too passive a metaphor, for the journey-like or dream-like aspects of the art process come to the fore, and the artist has within him more the myth of the hero than the archetype of the mother.

To return to the term "artistic causality," one of our graduate students has observed a subtle difference between a preschool child's spontaneous drawing of a man and a "demand" drawing of a man which she requests.[9] The latter, done for the "draw-a-man-lady," appears to be restricted and unintegrated compared with the former. It is as though already at this early age, often preceding recognizable man-schemas, the agency of the artist has been usurped.

By "idiosyncratic meaning" I refer to the affective and image-bound meaning which impels and guides the artist. I know that my terminology will meet with disapproval in some quarters, but I need a way to emphasize the subjective, uniquely-bound-to-this-one-life, situational aspects of making art. The term contains dissonant elements because I accept that even the collective and archetypical contents of the artist's mind enter idiosyncratically into the artistic process. As such, I take issue with Jung's demarcation between what he calls "psychological" and "visionary" artistic modes,[10] for I would make a distinction in degree and not in kind here, nor would I enter into as elaborate a construction of differences between conscious and unconscious processes, even while paying homage to the usefulness of these distinctions within Jung's system of psychology. (We will have reason to return to Jung later.) As with Read,[11] and others, I merely mean to treat the symbolic life of the artist as a search for "the forms of things unknown," a search which is guided by what I call idiosyncratic meaning. Without this ingredient, artistic causality has little to defend it from the incursions and designs of outsiders. This is why Lowenfeld so inveighed against imitation and coloring books.[12] His reasons were sound, for there is no art where artistic causality and idiosyncratic meaning are nonexistent. But the objects of his attack were an error, for I have seen individuals who have intended to copy or imitate, or even use coloring books, where these two principles were not denied.*

By "intentional symbolization" I refer to the artist's desire to work over into materials some equivalent of his idiosyncratic meaning. I believe this operates through the artist's effort to treat properties of medium in-process as an "*ad hoc* set of signs"[13] which he can analogically lead back toward the base in feeling or imagery which is his impetus. I use the term "lead back" advisedly, for the artist moves away from the collective properties or conventions of medium usage, or at the least submits these to the test of personal relevance. The communicative zone of an art work would seem to expand and contract with the degree of training and experience of the artist. In this sense, the novice is beneath the readily communicable collective traditions of medium usage, the successful professional is above them. Both, then, must enter into what I have called the "*ad hoc*" treatment

*Here I draw upon personal experience in the "drawing laboratory," where I have been doing longitudinal case studies of individuals doing a series of drawings. One boy drew from a wallet photograph for most of a ten-week series, giving ample evidence of mastering technical and affective goals he set himself. A girl tried to reproduce on scratchboard a blowup of "Snoopy" dancing. Case material, too voluminous to cite here, gives evidence in this case also that the artist's causality, idiosyncratic meaning, and intentional symbolization were operative. Examples of how such interpretations can be justified will appear in later chapters.

of medium in order to synthesize the situational aspects of each unique art process with artistic causality and idiosyncratic meaning. Medium, chance, interruptions, influences—all are a part of the "otherness" which makes each art process unique, alive, and unpredictable. Here, again, the very young child, before representational mastery leading to some reading of his efforts by others, already exhibits signs of intentional symbolization.[14] What is of interest to me here is that this intention is not dependent on the evolution of "diagrams, combines, and aggregates," which in Kellogg's formal taxonomy are claimed to precede not only "pictorials" but the intention to represent.[15] Not so, apparently, for the child intends to symbolize where we can only read a scribble, or he will make forms which invite such symbolization but will not be so interpreted by him for lack of intention, or he will give evidence of the potential for symbolic interpretation his efforts possess by fluently changing the meanings he applies to them. All would seem to be a part of the basic ability for symbolic transformation which Langer suggests precedes the development of language in the child.[16]

By introducing such terms as I have thus far, I hope to clarify some of the assumptions I bring to this book. Philosophically, I take a position much like that of the later Wittgenstein, who described art as a game whose rules are made up as the game is in progress, where the exact meaning of words or images is known only in the context of each new statement or articulation.[17] Such a view does not deny that regularities and commonalities can be teased out of several works, if one is so inclined. It merely proclaims the situational uniqueness of each art process as an essential aspect of its character.

In this book I concentrate on the active production of art, on the process of making art. The literature on the psychology of art and much of aesthetics bypasses this active focus. Lacking such a concentration, I will contend that much of art education and its research has been deflected into trivial or surface considerations. I will not impugn all existing efforts to study other aspects of art, but I will call into question their failure to live up to the promise of giving us greater insight into the art process itself.

It is also important to further delineate the assumptions upon which I proceed because, as a recent anthologist has indicated, it is open to question whether one can develop a purely psychological theory of art because so many conceptualizations about the nature of art will intrude upon him.[18] Any researcher, therefore, operates explicitly or tacitly from some kind of aesthetic theory.

More than that, so basic a realm of man's experience as art has around it inescapable mythic lore that operates, consciously or not, upon the individual artist. This means that though the artist may be socialized to a degree by his training and by artistic conventions and history, he will not be fully tamed or he will transgress against the hero myth, the journey into darkness or light, the conquest of unconscious forces, the renewal and transcendence, the embodiment of the archetype and of the revelatory and prophetic, which accrues by mythic inheritance to the role of the artist. I accept this lore, as I do the newer lore of creativity and self-actualization, as important forces and conceptualizations acting upon the artist in action. In a very real sense, to borrow a pregnant phrase from Jung, the artist can only "live the myth onward."[19]

Yet, while there is mythic lore surrounding the artist, there are no binding collective myths directly upon him, so that he is thrown back upon a kind of a "culte de moi," or upon exploration within his own life and psyche of whatever mythic remnants and archetypes he can there unearth. It is partially for this reason that the idiographic and morphogenic focus in research, (using Allport's terms[20]) is adopted in what is to follow. The fusion of the idiosyncratic and the collective, the intuitive and the logical in the art process can only be read, I assume, in the individual life. Even there it can only be partially and problematically approached under special conditions and means, some of which we hope to show as this book develops.

Such an approach as here attempted is indeed a humble one. A certain principle of noninflatability of interpretations must be invoked. I cannot claim to save art education by my efforts. It is enough, perhaps, to proceed with honesty, questioning, and trembling. It is reflexive research in art education that I invoke, much in the spirit of Gouldner's reflexive sociology.[21] I am concerned with how my research changes those I study, in fact, how it may be an ingredient in their artistic advancement; and I am concerned with how it changes me—with how it integrates the mythic, the philosophical, the psychological, and the empirical in my own mind. Just as I want my study to lead the artist on, I want it to lead my own thinking on. As the reader will soon learn, I attempt to dissolve the researcher-subject stance and the claim for superior objective-mindedness on my part. I study phenomena which are covert and nonverifiable, in the main, but which nonetheless have contingencies with the empirical world of description, first-person-singular statements of the artist, and participant-observation. Understanding and not prediction and control are my aim, and I search out events and interpretations of them which change man and his art, as opposed to statistical regularities based upon a misplaced naturalistic philosophy. My efforts are more toward structural and interpretive validity than what Pepper calls "multiplicative" verification.[22]

Further, the assumptions which I have been delineating will not allow me to espouse a behavioristic, operationally based, publicly verifiable methodology. Part of the motivation of this book is to explore alternatives to the overwhelming behavioristic model with its imperialistic world view of objective-mindedness which shrinks our image of man, "thingafying" him on the one hand, and pacifying him toward political, institutional, and technological manipulation on the other. It is indeed easier to explore the moon than our own minds. But for the latter, surely the making of art offers us an exemplary model of man at his most human and most generative level. (Langer, in fact, has used the art process as a means for explicating her concept of "mind."[23])

It is likewise true that the assumptions I have presented place the art process back in the hands of the artist, not in those of the researcher or the teacher. Whatever controls and influences the researcher and teacher may exert, to the extent they usurp the artist's causality, his idiosyncratic meaning and his intentional symbolization—nay, to the extent they dispel the mythic lore surrounding his concepts of art, or level out the uniqueness and "otherness" of each art process—to that same extent they have closed off from themselves as researcher and teacher the very thing they want to study and enhance. I am therefore left in th midst of a "humanistic psychology" which is concerned about the human uses of knowledge and about the impact of "methods" and interactions upon the phenomena one studies. The purpose of inquiry is thus crucial, and it is necessary to ask whether what is done aids the artist, for the researcher and the teacher must in parallel fashion participate in the mythic and life-enhancing movement which is essential to making art or their efforts become reductive of the very phenomenon into which they inquire or attempt to nurture.

"Methods" as such, seen as *a priori* determinations of what one should do or as a skein of systematic samplings based on a metaphysic of what Bridgman calls "the sufficiency of sub-atomic analysis,"[24] intrude to disintegrate what is a psychic, not a naturalistic phenomenon. The former will not allow us to tick off its objective components like isolated properties of natural objects which we seek in some way to control through our knowledge. (Even in the latter case, I acknowledge the purer motivation toward understanding which is part of the traditional ethic of natural science as well. Here I am merely trying to indicate an essential difference when man studies himself.)

I come to this task, then, as the result of my own experience and convictions in research.[25] What I propose to explore here is the next best step I can conceive of taking. Should it be of any use, even to the extent of drawing out more viable alternatives to my alternatives, I will be content. I may indeed fail in my efforts, for I am not attempting to borrow or adjust methods from other disciplines nor look to them to solve our problems or do our research. I have tried that route and, while I am not opposed to it, it is a time in my life to strike out on my own. There is no intention here to talk toward practical concerns (e.g., those of how art exists in the public schools) other than that most practical concern of enhancing our knowledge and zest for art and life.

Philosophically, this meager beginning is intended to reunite the subjective-objective split permeating inquiry into art, to transcend it, hopefully. As Fetter has put it:

> We are the being concerned with our own meaning. It is for the "humanities" to explicate and articulate what science cannot: man's relationship to being; how, and what it means, to be.[26]

Methodology and the "Roshomon" Effect as Seen from a Focus on the Drawing Process and the Drawing Series

2

That language can effectively cope with aesthetic phenomena is open to question. The aesthetic, defined as immediate (not mediated) and sensuous,[1] is indeed a part of "mind" (or consciousness) but is other than intellection, which proceeds by way of symbols and reflectively abstracts (or imposes) forms upon the immediately given. All research, thus, is abstract in one sense or another, as is all reflective thought.

Much of artistic behavior is accessible to standard social science research techniques. Drawings, for example, collected from samples of some defined population, can be submitted to certain kinds of judgment, scaling, and analysis. The Goodenough-Harris Draw-a-Man Test represents a controlled procedure for obtaining and scoring drawings of a man made by children of specified ages, yielding a scale score indicative of an individual's intellectual maturity according to age and sex norms.[2] Although this test purports to have no direct relationship to artistic behavior, it is obvious that similar techniques could be used to inquire into a child's ability, for example, to utilize the conventions of space as developed in Western representational art. (Eisner has done such a study.[3]) Or, again, setting up a criterion of artistic "expertise," it is possible for Child to describe the development of children's "aesthetic preference" and "aesthetic judgment," as operationally defined through selection from a series of pairs of slides of paintings those which match the experts' choice.[4]

I have no quarrel with such studies, provided they are seen for what they are. All too often, however, they are made the basis for interpretations and recommendations that touch more centrally the nature of artistic and aesthetic experience. The aesthetic and the artistic are not a matter of nose-counting. By definition they are locked in the particular, in the situational, in the experience of the "live creature." The aesthetic, to the person involved with it, is phenomenological, and not philosophical.[5] Expression, or the art process, likewise is indissolubly individual and unique, as I tried to show in the first chapter.

Inquiry into art, therefore, is in a peculiar position, insofar as it attempts in discursive form to come to grips with what is unitary and individual—that is, the closer it comes to art experience. In chapter 1, following Dewey, I tried to suggest that all experience is guided by something like an aesthetic consideration, by a "pervasive quality" which, further, stains efforts at analysis or description. Or, the thinker can reflect one situation upon another, which, as its ground, now becomes the organizer of what can be abstracted concerning the first situation (which then becomes an "object" of thought).

Sensitivity in inquiry into art, then, would seem to depend on closeness to that expressive or aesthetic situation or group of situations which it seeks to describe. But description, as Collingwood has pointed out, generalizes, whereas expression individualizes.[6] This is like saying that we are asked to generalize about things which cannot be generalized except at the expense of contradicting their essential character. This problem and paradox will linger behind everything I have to say in this book. At bottom, it cannot be dissipated. My aim is to make our inquiry sensitive to this paradox in a way that helps us as artists, researchers, and fellow human beings.

It is not my aim to catalogue traditional research methods, whether so-called empirical, philosophical, historical, or whatever. Numerous and detailed accounts of these are available already in a better form than I could supply, even if I wanted to. Nor do I intend to show how the methods described in these books could be applied to the subject matter and problems of art education, useful as this might be. So doing, would, I believe, perpetuate the existing condition of our research and ignore the paradox I have just indicated.

In the traditional view of natural science, a great many observational and descriptive studies precede controlled mathematical and experimental methods. It has been said that the sciences of man have not done this careful and patient groundwork. To that end, exhortations to researchers in art education to return to the phenomena of interest and to proceed by simpler observational and descriptive methods are well conceived.[7] When such methods are recommended, however, it is in the belief that variables will eventually emerge for mathematization and controlled experimentation, or at least that matters will tend toward that idealized state of affairs.

I do not any longer believe that knowledge about the artistic and the aesthetic will accumulate and evolve toward control in this fashion. Perhaps, as Langer has suggested, part of psychological science may tend more toward the physical and the biological, while another, considerable part may not fit our usual concept of "science" at all.[8] It may, she says, be more like history, or jurisprudence—it may, in other words, not tend toward the idealized, formalized, mathematized logical and mechanistic models we have inherited in the name of science and applied willy-nilly to the study of all aspects of man.

Steele, a research assistant who worked with me between 1967 and 1971, has recently proposed "a theoretical basis for understanding an individual's making of art."[9] The word "understanding" is used advisedly, in preference to "describing." The latter has a more definite and veridical ring to it, and suggests "generalizing" over "apprehending." "Understanding," further, has no connotation of predicting or controlling about it. Yet, beyond empathy, it allows for grasping of patterns and structural relationships, usually held together by some qualitative grasp of "wholeness." It has also a strong *a posteriori* ring to it. As such, it represents an attitude more congenial to the effort of connecting "knowing" with "art."

Steele presents a model[10] which looks like the one on page 8.

The middle portion of the model is my focus: theoretical knowledge of concrete particularizing givens. And since the knowledge of which I speak is that of art, the focus is upon knowledge of the uniqueness of such expressive situation, and of each history of expressive situations. What else, indeed, is art education concerned with? My usage is meant to encompass the appreciative situation as well, for in the latter case we are concerned with knowledge of the uniqueness of each relationship with art, in the existential sense.

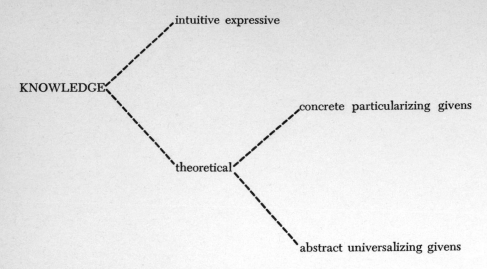

intuitive expressive

KNOWLEDGE

concrete particularizing givens

theoretical

abstract universalizing givens

Collingwood in his discussion of history offers some penetrating concepts concerning expression and history.[11] First, he states that the artist is not reflectively aware of his problem until after his work is done. It is at that point where it is possible to make a transition between unreflective (process-centered, on-going, clarifying) thought and reflective thought. There is, he says, no history of artistic problems, as such, as there is a history of scientific or philosophical problems. (The issue of continuity and tradition in art is not raised at this point.) By taking this position, Collingwood brings artistic problems down to their genuine base, that of the movement into individual form, or to expression, which individualizes instead of generalizing.

History, like biography, vacillates between interpretation and generalizing on the one hand and expression (individualizing, forming, being) on the other. The historian, when he tries to breathe life into the past, searches and sifts for evidence which he strives to fit together in a meaningful way. But there is a problem here, which Gombrich describes thus:

> There is much to be admired in this effort of the imaginative historian to "wake the dead" and to unriddle the mute language of the monuments. But he should never conceal from himself that his method is circular. The physiognomic unity of past ages which he reads from their various manifestations is precisely the unity to which the rules of his game have committed him. It was he who unified the clues in order to make sense of them.[12]

I take Gombrich to be saying that such "life" and "unity" is partly projective or at least a function of a perceiver who grasps unity as patterns and forms among clues. The "clues" of which we speak in the effort to arrive at knowledge of expression (or appreciation) are interhuman intuitions, patterns, influences not degradable to the reductionistic methods useful for knowledge of the general through abstract universals and formal operations. If there is a method here, it is, to borrow again Allport's words, "idiographic" and "morphogenic," but it is so through the perception of one person intent on knowing, who is also interacting with the phenomena of the expresive situation of another person. As with historical interpretation, it could always be otherwise given a change of historian or biographer and a resultant shift in clues. (In this sense we deal with a knowledge which cannot even presume to suggest that it transcends the human condition.) The mission of such knowledge is close to that proposed by Gouldner for a reflexive sociology:

". . . the task of helping men in their struggle to take possession of what is theirs—society and culture—and of aiding them to know who they are and what they may want."[13]

At this point, I have come close to what I have called in the title of this chapter the "Roshomon" effect. This is a meaning borrowed from the Japanese movie where the same "incidents" are related from three different points of view. I am inviting methodologically for the study of expression and appreciation as unique life situations a similar approach to that of the movie "Roshomon." Let the accounts of the unique proliferate, and let the viewpoint of the person reporting define his own relation (unavoidable, though called "contamination" in some behavioral studies) to the events he is trying to understand. If I were a virtuoso or if, indeed, I thought it posible, I would present three versions of a given expressive situation myself. My own perception and development are such that I suspect I can only give one account. Perhaps someone else will have greater virtuosity or see whether or not, apart from pure literature (an expressive situation itself) such an approach is possible.

It is possible, of course, to aim at knowledge of the general (through abstract universals, formalization, etc.) of some defined sample of artistic occasions. In earlier studies the art occasion has been defined by presence of media, a given task, a known sample from a defined population, various controls, treatments, etc.[14] Note that I have already changed my language. I spoke of knowledge of "a sample of occasions," not of knowledge of expression. The outcomes of this generalizing effort are not useless or untrue; rather, they are pale reflections almost out of touch with man's artistic life, and under a world-view of objective-mindedness they tend to be reductive of man's artistic life itself. Hence the need for alternatives. The early study of the creative process by Patrick[15] was unique for its time, but subsequent studies of similar orientation have failed to increase our insight into art expression. The assumption that there are interesting and useful regularities over diverse expressive situations has not paid off. It is just possible that there are more interesting and useful uniquenesses from one situation to another. Or perhaps the binding power between expressive situations is best seen within the series of a given individual.[16] At least this would seem more closely related to the experiential reality of art, and the unique patterns perceived and presented would perhaps increase our love for art and life. So it has been with me.

Nose-counting is a great leveler. Art breaks away from the level. Nature itself is prolific of individuals but still we come away with a clear perception of forms, of types. Perhaps, even, perceived structure in a unique setting will strike us as the exemplary case, as the unifying image. Such, at least, is Arnheim's claim in the distinction he draws between "type concepts" (those grasped by way of structure and unity) and "container concepts" (those constructed by means of criteria, by inclusion of categorical parts, etc.).[17]

In the above paragraph I am hinting at the fact that in the alternatives I suggest a different kind of "abstraction" is the result. These alternatives are frightening because they lack the security of an unquestioned method, supported in our culture but to a degree out of proportion to its merit in application to the broadest range of human affairs and experience. The errors to which my alternatives are prone are all too transparent to the critic. The errors to which a single, abstract, generalizing method is prone in relation to knowledge of art are concealed, doubtlessly, to the same critic.

It has lately become more apparent to me why art educators such as Lowenfeld[18] and Schaeffer-Simmern[19] have pressed back upon my consciousness. These men had "points of view." They were human, fallible, "unscientific" in that narrower sense, but above all they not only believed in art and its meaning for self-identity, but also interacted strongly with those experiencing art, immersing themselves within the ongoing art processes of specific individuals. Their "abstractions" and "theories" are a lived interpretation of their own experiences and, at longer view, the "contamination" we earlier rightly saw turns out to be a strength rather than a weakness, for it is a function of their own perception opposite the individual and unique nature of expressive situations.

And both men proceeded by way of empathic identification with an individual's base, a diagnosis, a clinical kind of "treatment" or method of nurturance, then a reading of direction and change from that person's base. They entered into the reality they described, learning to interpret departures and emergences from the unique context established for each individual.

At the time, none of my generation thought of this as "research." Seen as knowledge of expression, as I have been attempting to present it, I find it much easier to think of it as sensitive research now. My only change in emphasis would be that of interacting with less "treatment," or, consciously, none at all (a non-treatment treatment), so that the agency returns more centrally to the artist. (I make allowance for the work done with young children and those in therapy, although even here we do not know clearly what alternatives to the methods of these men might succeed as well, or better.) My emphasis, thus, is meant to be an alternative to charisma (the psychology of influence, of master-apprentice) and to materialistic, technological or behavioristic control (the psychology of fear and conditioning, of master-slave). I am closer, however, to the former than to the latter.

Mention of Lowenfeld and Schaeffer-Simmern bring me to another concept basic to this book. There is a kind of subjectiveness in the most "objective" of methods of research. As has already been hinted at, this has to do with the perspective through which we approach the object of study. As Frankl puts it, the thing we are searching for is in some way presupposed all along.[20] There are assumptions, presuppositions underlying one's search even before beginning it. So, while every description is from a limited perspective, nevertheless what is seen through that perspective can have theoretical and transsubjective meaning. Moreover, it can be useful to us, even though we must take the perspective into account.

How can it be useful to us? For one thing, it can extensionalize, literally string out, examples of the concrete givens, the unique situations which represent the endless variety of aesthetic occasions. As such, as we mature, we learn not to treat abstractly any artistic situation, except as our entering concepts, which we cannot avoid, become expectations brought to consciousness for disconfirmation in the present. Only so are we sensitive to our own art experiences or to those of another.

In addition, there is a sense in which the presuppositions of the researcher need to be seen as more than a bias. In a sense they make meaning possible to him. This is as true of a strict behaviorism as it is an approach more like the one being developed here. My quarrel with behaviorism is that the philosophical presuppositions underlying it have not been consciously examined by many who use its methods. And conclusions drawn from narrowly behavioristic studies have been accepted without regard to such limitations. An example illustrative of the reductionism prevalent in our habitual attitude toward science comes from Frankl, in his discussion of "dimensional analysis" (by which he refers to the fact that situations allow for a variety of interpretations, none of which may be in error, but some of which leave out a great deal, often without acknowledging that there is more to be considered).[21] It would be proper, he says, for a psychiatrist to refer to Joan of Arc as a schizophrenic but to refer to her as *nothing but* a schizophrenic represents a dangerous reductionism.

We have inherited a viewpoint concerning psychology paralleling our notions of science in its descriptions of "things." Dissection, manipulation, simulation are a part of the drive toward complete rational knowledge of things, as Fromm points out. But we cannot approach man in this way.

> Psychology can show us what man is *not*. It cannot tell us what man, each one of us, *is*. The soul of man, the unique core of each individual, can never be grasped and described adequately. It can be "known" only inasmuch as it is not misconceived. The legitimate aim of psychology thus is the negative, the removal of distortions and illusions, not the positive, the full and complete knowledge of a human being.[22]

Still further, Fromm delineates the problem upon me in my effort to break out of traditional empirical inquiry into alternative approaches:

> . . . we might speak of a "negative psychology," and furthermore say that full knowledge of man by thought is impossible, and that full "knowledge" can occur only in the act of love. Just as mysticism is a logical consequence of negative theology, love is the logical consequence of negative psychology.[23]

I accept this concept of Fromm's as one particularly true in our effort to know man (although I would qualify his position and suggest that *full* knowledge of any *thing*, by thought is impossible). Fromm is right, partially, because the self is likewise impossible to grasp or know. It is in living relation that the self and the other are intuitively grasped.

In research parlance, I can illustrate the above by extending Barker's concept of kinds of data.[24] He refers to O-data, or operator-data, as that wherein the psychologist talks to himself, as it were, through his operations. He constrains, that is, the form of the data by the questions he asks and the procedures and instrumentation he applies. The experiment exemplifies this orientation. T-data, or transducer-data, is that wherein the psychologist himself is a sensing agent, translating phenomena as they occur into signs. The field notes of the anthropologist might qualify as T-data. The extension occurs, however, as soon as we speak of a "participant observer" and try to delineate just what participation means. If participation transcends the "negative psychology" of which Fromm speaks and moves toward "love," as a transcendance of both self and other for "full knowledge," then, if we have data at all, we have what, following Buber, might be called D-data, dialogue-data (or encounter-data). Perhaps the word "data" seems out of place here, yet the etymology of the word allows it—it is, indeed, a "gift."

I need to digress a moment to set the stage for what is to follow. Buber speaks of a "duality" which is present in every "essential living relation" and which is transcended, completed, or transfigured therein. It is the dialogue, the living relationship of the self, to things, men, and mystery that bring about art, love, and religion.[25]

As we inquire into the making of art we can assume a perspective which treats the relationship of the artist to things (process, medium, situation) anywhere along a continuum from the O-data to the T-data to the D-data. None of these perspectives is wrong in itself. Likewise, none of them is reducible to another. To leave out the last view, which approaches the artist as though he is involved in a genuine dialogue in the art situation, would be most deleterious of all. Usually this is done by default, or, as often happens, it is assumed that the art situation is *nothing but* what is learned through O-data or T-data.

But the dialogue between a man and his evolving art work is existentially real to him foremost. He has privileged access to that encounter, and the psyhic phenomena pertaining thereto are only in unknown degrees sharable with another through first-person-statements coming from him, as artist. It is my contention that this kind of sharing is extraordinarily subtle, fragile, and problematic, and that it takes a relationship close to the end Fromm terms "love" to share it. In other words, the art dialogue and the human dialogue cross, the latter taking the former as its subject. In so doing, however, the kind of understanding arrived at will not submit to direct formulation, manipulation, and interpretation, as will O-data and T-data. The person entering this relationship from the side of inquiry will, if he attempts later to develop "theoretical knowledge of concrete particularizing givens" (as the model from Steele presented earlier puts it), perforce leave much unsaid, for indeed it is unsayable. The inquirer might attempt to deal with his understanding intuitively, which here would mean expressively, in the manner of art itself.

When I read analysts, therapists, depth psychologists, I find a model close to the present need. These men sense the difficulties to which I allude. Jung, for example, points out how abstract knowledge about man must be set aside when understanding is the therapist's or doctor's goal. Then it is the unique, the irregular which must press forward. In fact, he says, if treatment is schematic, the progress of the cure is jeopardized. He stresses that "the task of the doctor consists in treating the sick person, not an abstract illness."[26]

Jung further suggests that the more psychology concentrates on the individual, the more useful and lively the resultant knowledge will be. But this enviable result is bought at the cost of complexity, uncertainty, and the chance of error, a cost that academic psychology has largely been unwilling to pay.[27] The therapist, on the other hand, must often approach the patient as a counsel for his own (the patient's) defense. The individual case absorbs the therapist more and more, with the result that "the deeper his understanding penetrates, the more . . . general principles lose their meaning." As what to both parties feels like "understanding" increases,

> the situation becomes increasingly subjectivized. What was advantage to begin with threatens to turn into a dangerous disadvantage. Subjectivation (in technical terms, transference and countertransference) creates isolation from the environment, a social limitation which neither party wishes for but which invariably sets in when understanding predominates and is no longer balanced by knowledge. An ideal understanding would ultimately result in each party's unthinkingly going along with the other's experience. . . . It is therefore advisable to carry understanding only to the point where the balance between understanding and knowledge is reached, for understanding at all costs is injurious to both partners.[28]

I have dwelt on Jung's insights because he addresses directly the topic of the tension between understanding (the subjective identity between two persons whose complete individuality is maintained) and knowledge (the theoretical, the abstract, the interpretative). I believe that inquiry into the making of art is in a less precarious position than therapy, because in the former we enter into dialogue with the artist concerning his artistic process at a level of abstraction already once removed from it. Thus the role differences between artist and researcher are respected, and the important question, "What is the knowledge for?" can be answered satisfactorily to both. The artist seeks knowledge that may lead him on, that may help him "dream the myth onward." The researcher seeks knowledge of the kinds of regularities within processes and between works that occur in the case of a given individual artist, and he is interested in whether or not further generalizations or interpretations can be justified.

In the more difficult therapeutic relationship, Jung answers the question of what knowledge and interpretation are for: they are to increase the patient's conquest of self and his direction in life. Thus the patient's interpretations of symbols, dreams, and the like, take priority over Jung's. Jung's own efforts at linkages and meanings are treated as hypotheses to be verified in this context.[29] Nevertheless, as one reads Jung, it is obvious both that he has clear presuppositions and also that he extends his own general knowledge of the things he studies. The form of this knowledge is not like that projected by academic psychology, but it remains, at least to this reader, a kind of knowledge, or wisdom, all the same.

The purpose of this book, then, and through it of research from its viewpoint, is to maintain and further meaningful dialogue on art education through a blend of understanding and knowledge of unique expressive situations. "Understanding" requires my effort at immersion in the existential flow of the expressive situation. "Knowledge" requires justification for interpretations and generalizations, even when the latter refer mostly to a continuity of differences or uniquenesses in expressive situations, or when the former refer mostly to family resemblances, themas, nested strategies, and the like, within a given individual's series of expressions.

Consonant with the primarily existential phenomenological stance with which I begin (and which best matches the search for "meaning" and "understanding" as used herein), it is the individual artist's own series of works and the setting in which they occur which constitutes the most reliable and valid "sample" of expressive situations for study. Within themselves (as Jung says of the dream series[30]), the works of an artist's series are the context which the artist himself supplies. Therein the *ad hoc* use of medium, the recurrence of themas and images, the inclusive plans and strategies by which he guides himself, the peculiar transformations of process feedback, the response to chance and accident, and the like are available for understanding and tentative description and interpretation. These reverberate one upon the other, structurally supporting each other like clues from within a partially destroyed ancient manuscript which is uninterpretable in single passages but progressively understandable as parts are reflected upon each other.[31]

Were I to focus on school settings at the start, I would likely be drawn away from the essential data base I here propose: the individual series of expressions in a given (but more private) setting. Instead it would be very easy to be attracted to the construction of a theory of art teaching, whereas I am more concerned with a theory of learning in art, or more properly still, of meaning in art. From the focus on the individual apart from the school, one may wish to go to the study of that same individual in the school setting. (From cases I can recall of unusual children and of quite "ordinary" adults, I would guess that the same individual's series in the school setting would often be a pitiable thing compared with his series in the untaught, nonclass setting.) More serious to my view is the climate engendered wherein the manipulanda of teacher and school and of research in that setting disintegrate or render opaque the very subject of inquiry: the making of art. Instead, the teacher's roles as custodian, preacher, therapist, and purveyor of cultural "chunks," and the student's institutional and social behavior and incidental learning absorb the researcher's attention, for it is these that I suspect are primarily operative in the public school. That reality indeed needs sensitive description and interpretation, too. (Perhaps in the manner of Smith and his co-workers, who approach this task as ethologists and participant observers, and of whom we will have more to say later.)[32] But I would no more go there to study the making of art than I would go to the zoo to study the normal behavior of animals. I might go to the schools to study how art is indeed being made in the schools, but I would prefer to have first a clearer conception of individual children's series of expressions where the ontological nature of the meaning they find in art and how they direct their series is the primary concern. In other words, I would first like to ascertain the kind of artistic causality, idiosyncratic meaning, and intentional symbolization present from this individual, limited-context perspective before launching on a study of probably more pathological or distorted conditions. There is no snobbishness or criticism intended in this view. A parallel statement would be that I would not begin a study of religious experience in the typical institutional church. In this sense, this book is a call to basics and to soul-searching, philosophically and methodologically.

As I have tried to indicate, I am sensitive to parodoxes I cannot completely resolve (for example, the particular and the general, understanding and knowledge, the "subjective" existential-experiential and the "objective" behavioristic). Perhaps the more kindly reader will sense more of a shift of emphasis than an out-and-out flight from tradition and our current somewhat moribund scientific cosmology. It is indeed funny how in a period of two decades I have run from the neglect of philosophic presuppositions and the shortcomings of anecdotal types of behavioral descriptions to a desire to center upon these. I can only take solace in having some distinguished company.

There is, however, a more general issue which can be discussed. Barker and Wright put it thus:

> Adequate conceptualization of a particular person's behavior and its conditions is possible only if one has both [the actual events and their context] before him for deliberate examination. A geologist cannot determine the full significance of a particular rock formation until he has placed it in relation to the geological structure of the surrounding region. Neither can a psychologist be expected to get the full meaning of a behavior unit until he has placed and studied it in the sequence and context to which it belongs.[33]

In other words, the meaning of a "behavior unit" must be seen within "the stream of behavior," as Barker terms it. To construct a parallel here may be useful. In studying expressive situations, we do not have aesthetic behavior units, for we have assumed that aesthetic experience is a psychic reality foremost. To borrow an earlier term from literary art, *we must contend with the psychic reality of aesthetic experience within the artist's stream of consciousness in the unique expressive situation.* This shift is as great as from day to night (and, indeed, the picture may look black at first view). Having so said, our interest does not depart from the more easily ascertainable "actual events and their context," as Barker puts it. But if the stream of consciousness is where the action is, that becomes our first concern.

A noted developmental psychologist visited the "drawing laboratory" where over the past four years I have been studying various individuals involved in a drawing series. He came for a number of consecutive times when the same individual was drawing. At first he recorded all the actual, phenomenal events in context and in time that he could—how, for example, the artist sat in thought, his posture, his attentiveness to occurrences around him in the lab, his apparent mood, etc. After several times, however, the psychologist admitted that such a running time-sample record while the artist was drawing was not "where it's at," that, indeed, the important occurrences were covert, internally mediated. (By the way, I should report that his observations of overt behavior were far from useless. They were just not nearly enough.) Even with preschoolers, as Dempsey has shown,[34] we need the series perspective, the context, and the preschooler's spontaneous verbalizations and verbal responses, for an essentially neutral observer to adequately grasp what has been done. The cross-sectional survey of drawings and the formal analysis of drawings are, again, not worthless but they are severely limited methods of study which pay a high price for their certitude in abstraction.

At first I thought that process records of drawings would yield great insight into the making of art. At one level of abstraction, this was true. Two fairly clear drawing strategies involving something akin to hierarchical plans for executing and organizing total drawings were described.[35] Although in the main mutually exclusive, these strategies could be manipulated, modified, influenced, and learned under varying conditions, some of which were teased out from controlled experiments.[36]

As so often happens in science, art, and life, the latent utility of my experimental environment eluded me. I utilized "process recall" stimulated by time-lapse photographs of the history of a given drawing as an independent variable that I could manipulate to affect drawing strategies. In so doing, I strove to operationally represent internally mediated processes as well as influences from the environment and from teaching. I left out the continuity between the drawings of any given individual. I left out the plans and intentions he might have or discover and treated him as essentially a source of error except as he conformed to his fellow cell-mates in response to their classification and their treatment. The manifest utility of such an approach is obvious. It enabled me to speak with certainty within the severe limitations of my experiments. It enabled me to improve from one experiment to the next, in craftsmanlike fashion. It brought me some rewards and recognition within the existent psychological research value system. It allowed me to entertain a long-range hope for the cumulative development of studies that would lead to construction of theories of learning and teaching in art.

Certainly we can study the impact of educational institutions and of teaching upon art, just as we can have a social history of art, or study how economic conditions impinge on artist and art. We can even study the effects of scientific research into art upon art. All such studies are not only legitimate but useful—but, just as the efforts to analytically determine criteria present within some criterion of "good" art have not been successful (because of the gestalt-like contextual and relational meaning of such criteria in any given work), so all of the above approaches have not funded toward any clearer conception of art and how it functions. For we do not deal with a concept determinable in this way. As Langer puts it, an art work is a whole held together only by activity, and as such is comprehensible foremost in the situation of articulation or of active perception of it.[37] All that relates to these situations is not psychic, but to return to our earlier principle, aesthetic experience is a psychic reality which we must seek for in the stream of consciousness participating in the unique expressive or actively responsive situation.

It is here that the latent utility of process recall has come to the fore. Having given the drawing back to the artist (where by our analysis it belongs, whatever the impingements upon it), process records still give us only shadowy insights into transformational acts, deflection or reinforcement of intentions, influence of chance and accident, and the like. For these, we need access to the artist's stream of covert events in the drawing situation. These are unobtainable by any direct means. Any efforts to have these reported during the drawing process have failed and intruded upon what we have accepted as a dialogue between artist and the developing work—a kind of lived dream affected by and transforming the tangible environment. Stimulated process-recall enables us to enter into the unique expressive situation as closely as we can without destroying it. The privileged access of the artist intent upon reflection on his own unique drawing situation is essential to the grasping of aesthetic experiential phenomena. We must, as I like to put it, read the future of a drawing as history. And, like history, we must place recalled and shared process events within the antecedent and consequent conditions which constitute the drawing series.

Even as Smith has learned in his attempt to describe the complexities of classroom settings in detail,[38] in the drawing process, seen in series perspective, we deal with issues of "continuity" (current events have pasts and futures which are projected), and with "ringmastership" (multiple and simultaneously occurring strands of which the artist is to some degree aware and which he variously tries to manipulate). The point is that the greater part of what occurs covertly in the stream of consciousness of the artist is unreadable from even process samples of the work. Between any two overt changes, as recorded by process records, come decisions and transformations, the latter often of a symbolic nature, not deducible from the beginning- and end-points under scrutiny.

For an example, let me relate in superficial fashion what occurred just recently in a series of drawings done within about an hour and a half by an untrained college student working in the drawing lab. He began intending to draw a marcher stepping out, holding a trumpet or similar instrument in outstretched arms. His effort at obtaining the desired stance failed and, though frustrated, he attended to what his beginning might match. It suggested a sleep-walker, so he left the arms outstretched without an instrument, put a stripe down the leg to suggest, for him, pajamas (although I could read it equally as "uniform"), and called it quits. This procedure of projecting an intention, failing, and out of frustration matching the given reality with a revised goal, was repeated over three more drawings (which I will not detail here). On the fifth drawing, he began with a large, block figure "1." (Was it suggested by the drawing numbers used to label the negative, by the sign "we're no. 1" at the last football game? He couldn't say for sure why he did it; apparently it was a more playful, less intentional start.) The right bottom base of the figure "1" was disproportionately larger than the left base, which disturbed him for its lack of symmetry. For no clear reason he could recall, he gave the figure an eye and a mouth, making it into a kind of block animal. This suggested to him a Chinese interlocking wooden puzzle he used to have which could make many things, including a dog. He added other pieces, failing in part to obtain the interlocking quality he sought. It also suggested the Trojan horse. He forgot the puzzle, shaded in the various segments as seemed good and varied to him, added ears and a nose, and called it finished.

Note that the last described drawing had a different "plan" (or "non-plan") behind it than the first four he did. It is quite possible that this related to the first four frustrated, rather specific initial intentions requiring a degree of mastery he did not succeed in obtaining. More importantly, both drawings described would yield a different means-ends process analysis (lacking the artist's recall and typically thinking from the end back) as compared with an in-process recall analysis (where intentions, evaluations, frustrations, transformations, and the like, are prime forces on the formative drawing field). In this simple example, minimal issues of continuity, ringmastership and the like are involved. Moreover, the issue of whether aesthetic experience is centrally involved does not seem pertinent to the description. Indeed, the latter is what I call an "emergence"—a byproduct which wafts along the on-going events.

The emphasis I have given by centering on the psychic nature of aesthetic experience is one intended to connect internal and external events, as they are indeed linked in the drawing process. The effort at correction of current research biases inclines me to overstress internal determinants and processes, but I am in accord that external proceedings, the context of the drawing lab and the interaction with my assistant and me as participant observers, are all influential in the drawing process. We will say more on this score later. The internal proceedings are overridingly important because without access to these the greater part of in-process data is lost to us or misinterpreted, and because neglect of such data usurps power, fantasy, and directionality properly pertaining to the artist and his process dialogue.

As soon as we concentrate on a climate wherein revelation of the artist's stream of consciousness as recalled in association with a unique expressive situation is possible, the myth of the artistic and the creative in the individual life is reinforced, for we have tacitly supported the possibility of the psychic and subjective reality of aesthetic experience in a given individual's life.

It would be well that I describe for the reader the context within which I have been studying an individual's drawing processes and drawing series. A private studio and drawing laboratory has been set up wherein an individual, typically a college undergraduate not majoring in art, can make any kind of drawing he pleases (including drawing from models, from mind, from other pictures, etc.) in black and white media (ink, paints, charcoal, Conté crayon, pencil, pen, brush, etc.). As he draws, time-lapse photographic records of his evolving drawing are taken at regular intervals by a camera out of sight trained on a front-surface mirror mounted at a forty-five degree angle over his head. The artist comes once a week, averaging between one and two hours weekly. He may come for ten weeks only, although some have come for twenty and some thirty weeks, with or without ten-week intervals (school terms) in between. Before each drawing session the room is darkened and the time-lapse records of the previous week's drawings are projected on the wall for a stimulated process recall and exploration of the drawing's evolution and any reflections pertinent thereto. My assistant and I feel free to ask non-leading questions to ascertain what took place. We try not to give evaluations, direction, or instruction. The student knows that he is to be self-taught and self-directed in the drawing lab, that he can bring in or ask for anything important to his work, and that we would like the right to question him concerning his drawing processes and concerning the relationship of one drawing to another. My assistant and I make "field notes" recalling observations, current drawing behavior, lab conditions, how the feedback (process recall) proceeded, etc. These short-hand recollections, insights, and interpretations are important for our own memory and continuity. We of course label products and process records. And we tape and convert to typescripts the inquiry and recall taking place during process feedback.

In terms of the earlier discussion in this chapter of O-data, T-data, and D-data, the following might be said of the above research format. The drawing lab and its presuppositions are a kind of unreadable O-data. By this I mean that the conditions, rituals, and actions taking place in the lab reinforce our notion that art is a dialogue between artist and evolving work, that we honor what I have called artistic causality, idiosyncratic meaning, intentional symbolization and the like. Were I involved in experimentation, I might test out whether this setting as compared with others did in fact transmit a set in keeping with the general conditions obtaining therein. For example, we could focus on an individual's series of drawings done in a drawing class, describing the setting, and related conditions there, and compare the processes, insights, series, and the like, occurring under the two conditions. This might be worth doing, but we have not done so.

Our lab could be looked upon, likewise, as O-data were we to do a content analysis of our inquiries with the artist, classifying our questions, amount of talk, subtle suggestions (whether intended or not), and the impact these may have had on the artist's processes and series. Or we could attempt to show that the greater the number of weeks a person spent in the lab, the better his drawings became by some external or trans-subjective judgment of goodness or learning. We could also see whether the artist developed a larger repertory of "art concepts," especially of what have been called "third-order concepts" (in this case concepts about one's concepts about making art).[39]

But our data are not centered on the above perspective, for while we admit to presuppositions and attempt to justify them, we accept these as necessary limitations to our empirical (yes, I still use the word) study of drawing processes and series. In this sense, we have no hidden agenda, and we are not consciously manipulating the environment in a systematic way. (We are also not treating persons as subjects or even objects in some experimental design wherein they appear as representatives of types and are given controlled treatments.)

Our data are, instead, T-data and D-data. The notes and tape-scripts and process records are T-data, but the cumulative insights, the steady drift toward understanding and identity with the artist as he shares his mind, his hopes, plans, fears, insights, and long-range goals—all of this drift is toward D-data, dialogue-data. This is data of the inter-human touching on the mythic. We are lost in it, as is the artist, until we back out and make our feeble efforts at interpretation and theory. And in this drift toward understanding, we see resurrected within the artist what I have called his own myth of self-identity—the feeling that he constructs and transforms a self along with his art.

From the more hard-nosed scientific view, we might hope to achieve something equivalent to Bridgman's individual "calculus of idiosyncratic words in the private mode" in art.[40] Thereby one might cumulate cases, as in medicine, so that we might more effectively conceive of others.[41] The words stick in my throat, for the analogy to medicine suggests "treat similar cases." For I feel foremost their dissimilarity. Perhaps the matter is closer to Jung's analogy earlier cited—the art teacher needs general knowledge (if this constitutes it) but he "treats" this artist, not a type or a problem case, or perhaps, as Campbell suggests of myths,[42] they may have similar forms over time, but the stimuli evoking them and their semantic content are forever new.

By focusing on the individual and his drawing series and on the context in which it occurs and by alluding to the emergence of the individual's myth of self-identity in relationship to drawing, we evoke that sense of interdependence and directionality that Murray suggests is characteristic of what he calls "serials."

> Many actions—though temporally discreet, are by no means functionally discreet; they are continuations of a shorter or longer series of preceding actions and are performed in the expectation of further actions of a similar sort in the future. Of this nature are skill-learning activities, and behaviors which are oriented toward some distant goal, a goal which cannot be reached without months or years of effort. Also to be included here are the behaviors which form part of an enduring friendship or marriage. Such an intermittent series of proceedings, each of which is related dynamically to the last and yet separated from it by an interval of time for recuperation and the exercise of other functions, may be termed a serial.[43]

Murray goes on to say that serials suggest behavior far removed from the old S-R (Stimulus-Response) formula. He uses the term, therefore, *proaction* in contrast to *reaction* to refer to an action initiated spontaneously from within. He says, further, that proaction does not attempt to arrive at homeostasis, but that it is rather *superstatic*, since it adds something new to a previous condition. Significantly, he adds:

The integrates of serials, of plans, strategies, and intended proactions directed toward distal goals constitute a large portion of the ego system, the establishment of
personality which inhibits irrelevant impulses and renounces courses of action that
interfere with progress along the elected paths of life.[44]

Murray says that most people are in the midst of several on-going serials and that
they turn their minds and efforts to these when circumstances permit. I feel that
the concept I am trying to develop concerning the drawing series has much of the
characteristic of Murray's "serial" for the artist. It is a continuing dialogue, project,
and path. Following Murray's lead, and corroborating this from case material in
the drawing lab, how this "artistic serial" intertwines and interacts with other
serials in an individual's life provides further insight into the drawing series itself.
Quite often, as indicated by many observers, the artistic serial, concerned with
self-identity and self-transformation, has a spread-effect upon other aspects of
life—for example, upon one's self-confidence and upon his general sensibilities.
No claims are made for this here, but it remains a possible consequence of such
serials.

Overview of Alternatives to Be Presented

The larger part of the remainder of this volume will be devoted to alternative
methods of research which it is hoped will assist in bringing more meaningful and
vital dialogue back into art education. The approaches presented are not exhaustive
of all those possible; rather, they represent those which I find most challenging and
most basic for understanding the making of art, with an eye on the unique expressive situation, its context, and the artistic serial of which it is a part. Since my purpose is nothing short of a complete reexamination and reorientation of our research
presuppositions and procedures, I realize that it is with considerable brashness or
foolhardiness that I begin my task. As suggested before, I am banking on the
belief that the self-reflexiveness and the change of heart that have gradually come
upon me are shared by many others in the field, young and old alike.

It is questionable whether I should even refer to the alternatives to follow as
"methods," at least as contrasted to the usual connotation of that term in research
texts and courses. I am more concerned with orientations, their justification, and
their utility in furthering our knowledge and understanding of the making of art.
I will attempt to be persuasive in my explication of the alternatives, but I will
make no claim toward completeness nor toward the full detailing of working procedures.

All of the alternatives rest on two rather clear assumptions. *The first is that so-
called mentalistic concepts are essential to the study of the making of art.* My basic
principle, discussed earlier, goes much further, however, than do those liberal
cognitive psychologists admitting to their perspectives such terms as imagery,
intention, and the like, for I have indicated that I conceive of aesthetic experience
as a unitless psychic reality attendant upon, or emergent from, the artist's stream of
consciousness in the unique expressive situation. Further, the making of art is best
understood within a perspective of continuity. The series, or the artistic serial, links
meanings and means through time, with all the reverberations of events along a
path. If we focus upon individual cases, there arises that tension between idiosyncratic and collective meanings that gives the artistic serial the quality of a
mythogenetic journey.

*The second assumption is that as researchers we must act as special participant
observers if we are to gain access to the internal events and the guidance system
at work in the unique expressive situation,* and, to repeat, we must reflect the latter

within a serial and a contextual perspective. The participant observer method is specialized and unique in the study of the making of art because the mentalistic phenomena we must penetrate are privileged and partially unsharable even under the good intent to share (because non-verbal, not fully conscious, and the like). Further, since there is no direct access to the stream of consciousness operating within the unique expressive situation, all of the covert or internal material with which we deal as special participant observers is inferred, indirect, and tentative, requiring empathy and intuition in addition to the cultivation of a climate of trust where sharing is possible and where it has its own special utility (as, for example, a dialogue wherein the artist reflects in order to project, thereby strengthening his peculiar artistic serial).

A participant observer stepping into this very real but very privately based world functions more as a nurturant friend than as a disciplined, self-conscious observer.[45] More than that, he must in his attitude convey the feeling that he grasps the mythogenetic quality of the art process and serial, so that, though his role is clearly toward understanding and knowledge, he is trusted by the artist as being truly non-manipulative and open. The feeling conveyed to the artist should permit the artist to trust the participant observer with the task of description and interpretation without feeling that the meaning of the occasion and series is exhausted thereby.

In areas of study such as art, the role of research should be to enhance and further the qualitative and human phenomena which are its concern. Only by so doing will research come to grips with what it attempts to understand. I prefer to start with the individual making art, then move to the complex formal art education setting. In the latter, too, that research is good research which by its very presence makes the mix of students, teachers, and the environment more productive according to the complex intentions operative in that setting. If through the role of a special participant observer feelings of obstructions, failures, and frustrations are shared, these should be necessary feedback for that system's self-correction. (The instance of possible pathological cases is postponed for later consideration.)

All of this is background for the alternatives to be presented. In further preparation, I would direct attention to the fact that the alternatives are so organized that they begin with the microuniverse of the single artist as the subject of inquiry and proceed to the macrouniverse of the complex formal art education setting, with its usual complement of teachers, students, special school environment, curriculum, institutional organization, and community forces. The latter is to be presented like the study of an ecological system, with the connotation that each system is unique and that it, too, like the individual artist, must be studied in depth over time. The role of the participant observer in the latter instance is more difficult to define, especially since competitive and political forces may render open sharing of intentions and thought processes within various levels of the system unlikely. Consideration of such problems, however, must await the full discussion of this alternative.

At its best, this microuniverse to macrouniverse continuum, still with its eye primarily on the making of art, represents, at its one pole, the art dialogue, and, closely linked thereto, the human dialogue of artist and participant observer. At the other pole, the art dialogue is still central, though in some danger of being vitiated by external forces; but to the extent that vital interhuman relationships obtain, there also exists a true human community. Here the interhuman element does not centrally include the participant observer, although he needs to be a true participant if he is to understand the meaning of community arising where there is true mutuality and sharing between the members of the groups.[46] The tendency at this end of the continuum is to explain away the art dialogue as "nothing but" the action of external forces upon the artist, and to a large extent this may be so, if the artistic serial with its reinforcement of causality, intentionality, and symbolic power arising from its own idiosyncratic base is drastically weakened.

The alternatives begin with a consideration of the single artist engaged in the making of art, but with an emphasis on presentational modes closest to the artist's own stream of consciousness. These will range from more expressive (literary) accounts to more historical accounts (but with minimal interpretation), all largely keyed to the artist's "subjective perspective." These modes will be discussed in chapter 3.

Chapter 4 will attempt to present modes of interpretation based on a historical perspective which connects the inferred and shared stream of consciousness of the working artist more closely with observable in-process events, series linkages, contextual impingements, and the like. These efforts will be less expressive and literary, more historical. Historical is taken to mean that questions will be asked, evidence sifted for answers, and interpretations offered on the basis of accumulated insights. Theory, to the extent it appears, will emphasize, as in the earlier model of forms of knowledge, "concrete particularizing givens." It will refer, that is, to a given artist's serial and its context. Generalizations would occur if cases were pooled, as in the medical case method analogy earlier cited. Without the pooling of cases, reference will be made to "speculations" rather than "generalizations."

Chapter 6 will shift toward what might be called the microethnography of complex formal art educational settings. The possible forms and outcomes of such inquiry will be discussed, although I will limit my attention largely to my avowed purpose of furthering vital dialogue on art education, and restrict myself to interpretations close to my major assumptions of the importance of the artist's stream of consciousness and of special participant observer methods which make sharing and furtherance of the artistic dialogue possible. The difference is that these will occur in this instance within a more complex institutional and interpersonal field than the examples of single artists at work.

Presentational Modes Close to the Artist's Stream of Consciousness

3

Congruent with my two major assumptions (the need for access to the artist's active stream of consciousness while making art, by means of a special participant observer relationship, through the indirect means of a stimulated process recall within a nurturant setting), and positioned toward the rarer extreme poles of the two continua described above (the microreality stressing the individual artist and what is called D-data), the alternative modes discussed in this chapter will seem to many readers closer to literature than to science. For this reason I have called them "presentational modes."

While I will try to make distinctions between the various modes to follow, it should be obvious that the lines drawn between them are arbitrary and tentative. At most, such distinctions as are drawn are to sensitize us to subtle nuances between modes, and to unique insights possible within each.

The understanding resulting from these modes is closer to appreciation, as we associate this term with the experience of art, than to a knowledge which has a stronger discursive and cognitive component. We seem to grasp through immersion in experience of a literary work both the existentially unique aesthetic or appreciative encounter and some residue which, in a strange sense, "generalizes" in our mind about "life," "man," "love," "art," and the like. We acknowledge to ourselves that we cannot place any defensible logical or discursive structure upon the latter residue, yet we persist in our belief that we have achieved a kind of insight, or a kind of intuitive knowledge. Thus, for the person utilizing the modes of this chapter, he is laboring like the artist more; and for the person responding, he is more like the appreciator. The difference between these modes and literature is largely that the events beneath the modes occurred within a real and not an imagined time and place. The situation, therefore, is more akin to biography than to fiction; although it is apparent that biographies themselves move, on the one hand, closer to fiction, and on the other, closer to the historical documentary.

When we aspire to indirect access to the creating artist's stream of consciousness, and when we acknowledge the human dialogue which makes this access honest and possible, we become immersed in psychic realities, potential and shared insights which we more or less construct and present, rather than merely categorize and describe. To this degree, work in most of the modes of this chapter is expressive, literary. I have preferred to call them "presentational" to connote subtly that the experience of the events, psychic, overt and dia-logic, is as direct and as related to time and context as possible. What we have, then, is a special kind of literature, or a special kind of biography.

I trust that it is not necessary at this point to justify these modes nor to persuade the reader that they are important. The reasons why I believe them to be have been presented in the first two chapters. To the extent that such approaches succeed, they will enhance our appreciation of art through their presentation of the uniqueness of each expressive act and context. Further, since we deal with the artistic serial, they will also enhance our appreciation of the unique path emergent from connected expressive acts over time, and of the mythogenetic quality of such a path. We may also appreciate that to grasp all of this we must be a part of it, and take responsibility for our indirect influence on its future. And finally, as in a novel, we may be left with a residue which encourages us to generalize tentatively about art and life. We would not expect to generate hypotheses from these modes, however, which would be subject to verification in some hypothetico-deductive system. In fact, none of the modes in this entire book has that end in view, for that end is inconsistent with the major assumptions put forward here. It is true that modes presented later permit progressive abstraction to the point where hypotheses may be generated for verification, but at that point we no longer deal with the reality of art in its experiential and contextual uniqueness, but with extra-art abstractable properties. I have no reason to denigrate such efforts, only to counter them with alternatives closer to my conception of a vital psychology of art. The abstractions I feel drawn to do not permit hypothetico-deductive experiments.

The organization of the modes which follow owes much to the thought of Steele,[1] who worked with me for three years in the drawing laboratory. He developed a number of "pattern types" which are the basis for my own efforts at elucidating presentational modes. (He should not be held accountable for the way I describe and evaluate these modes.)

Modes of Mute Evidence

Artists properly distrust verbalization about art, especially when it makes any pretensions toward explaining art or speaking abstractly about it. What is implied here is the belief that art speaks for itself, in its own presentational mode, in its own medium and project of articulation, and that no translation into some other medium or mode, as in discursive thought, is possible without completely changing its existential and presentational meaning.

Iconic Representations of the Expressive Situation

The expressive act and the behavior stream and context surrounding it can be represented in varying degrees of iconicity. A video-tape or motion picture film can record the setting and the observable overt acts of the artist as the work in question evolves. The film and T.V. have their own peculiar qualities as media, as is well acknowledged by practitioners. There is, for example, the subtle effect of camera angle and distance, of light, of movement of the camera, of lenses, of speed, and the like. In the case of film, multiple views of the same event can be "edited" into any number of variations. With a full T.V. studio's potential, the "mixing" of multiple views is possible. In any event, these media, in either simple or complex form, can represent the observable acts and the setting with a high degree of fidelity. Sounds occurring in the environment can be recorded to accompany the visual record.

Such representations may in themselves constitute interesting "documentaries," or they may be so done within their medium that they are themselves an art form. If an artistic serial is involved, as is the case in the drawings I am studying, the records become voluminous and repetitive, taking as much time to reexperience the events as when they transpired. Their utility for detailed study of overt acts and events, however, is unquestionable.

Process Representations of the Evolving Art Work

As indicated earlier, we have been sampling time-lapse still-photographs of drawings from a front-surfaced mirror mounted on a forty-five-degree angle over the drawing table. Such records, sampled either methodically or via an intuitive judgment of "significant noticeable change," faithfully reconstruct the metamorphoses or stages of development of a given drawing. Context and the overt acts of the artist are largely ignored, except as these appear through a focus on the drawing itself. These records, when spread before one, constitute another kind of mute evidence of the expressive act. Unlike film and T.V., they reconstruct the art process in a more abstract way, by way of time sampling and by way of excluding events outside the drawing.

Figure 1. Samples of time-lapse process records.

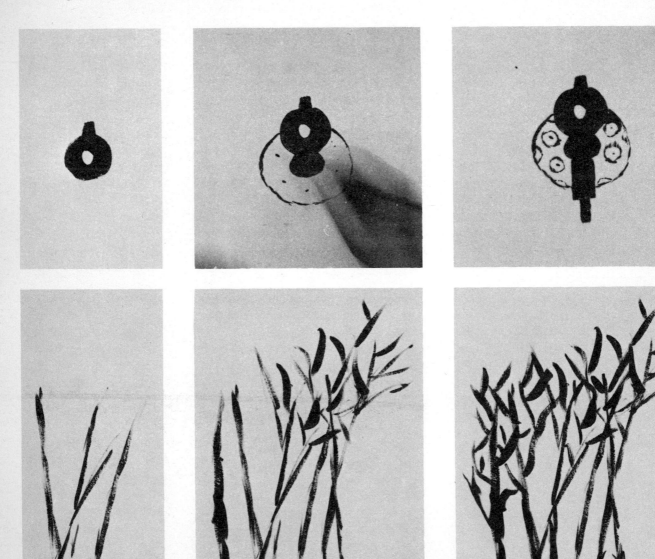

Since, again, I have been concerned with artistic serials, it is possible to represent a given series of drawings by the placement side by side of the different time-lapse drawing processes. More typically, the finished drawings themselves are taken to represent the series, and each of these is in turn backed up by the in-process samples. There is, of course, a medium effect in still photography also, but it seems less obtrusive than in film or T.V.

The examples above, termed "mute evidence," are in reality evidence only as they are used for some other purpose. In themselves, they are not really presentational modes related to the major assumptions of this book, for they do not contend with indirect access to the artist's stream of consciousness through a special participant observer. Mute evidence modes are assuredly useful within this special perspective, however, as indicated by the preferred and productive approach to the artist's privileged experience through stimulated process recall via works and time-lapse process records. The utility of process records for descriptions of commonalities across drawings (as in the earlier study of drawing strategies[2]) is obvious and undeniable, but that usage moves away from this book's focus on the unique expressive act and the unique artistic serial and the way our inquiry becomes a part of that. Figure 1 gives samples of time-lapse process records of two drawings by the same student.

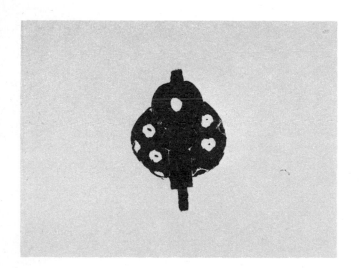
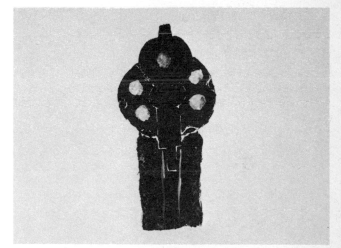

T-data Modes

As in the case of iconic representational modes, the verbal descriptions and transcriptions subsumed under this heading are meant to stand for the events they represent in as direct a fashion as possible. Because the term "T-data" is borrowed from Barker,[3] the reader is referred to his work for a fuller sense of how he uses it.

In essence, the observer, participant observer, or special participant observer, uses himself insofar as possible as a neutral sensing and recording instrument. One should not stress "neutral" too much, however, for the use of oneself as an instrument assumes that the bias in one's own perception is unavoidable and, perhaps, even useful. We do not observe other people, especially in the expressive situation, as though they are mindless automata in the grip of purely external stimulus conditions. Rather they appear to us as intentional, purposeful, and planful beings with a history and with a future. Further, as observers, we appear to ourselves, though obliquely, in the same manner.

And when we concern ourselves with the artistic serial, we soon learn how much of the expressive situation is covert and dependent, if we are to describe it, upon a history of shared insights and intuitions. Nevertheless, we can and do describe the "highlights" of our impressions of what transpires before us. The anthropologist writes his "field notes," or talks into a recorder for later transcription.

Figure 2. Frank's drawings

My assistant and I have over the past four years attempted to keep up diary entries or lab notes on each session in which an artist visits the drawing lab. Below are excerpts from one session occurring at week-9 of one undergraduate's work in the drawing lab. Frank, as I'll call him, is untrained in art. He is a premedical student. By week-9 (next to the last week of the usual term's work), the observers refer to the history in the lab, as well as what is right before them. They also risk interpretations and reveal their interests just by what they consider significant to record. Three examples follow. The first is my own. The second is that of a psychologist friend who observed Frank over a number of consecutive weeks in the lab. The third is by the graduate research assistant working with me. Figure 2 shows the drawings which Frank made during W-4, W-8, and W-9, which are referred to the lab notes.

Example 1, Frank _____, W-9, November 26, 1969, K.R.B.

John had put a lamp and a tree in his rain picture, but it didn't work out—didn't stay back in space, so he erased them.

He had intended to put in more people but just couldn't place them. He wanted the smaller figure to be further back in space than it turned out. He also had in mind a night scene, with street light, big yellow reflections. The puddles were added last to capture the rain idea. Not satisfied with these. Hands he can't do (or faces), so these were left out.

He made the association with the shark drawing (W-4), insofar as the spatial problem exists, but he didn't think of this at first. He was not pleased with the umbrella's position. It should have been angled more to suggest going into the wind.

He stopped us after last week's session and asked if we could identify the forms on steps and pavement, which I did, stating that they were puddles. "Correct," he said.

After viewing the sequence on the screen, he said that it was connected in his mind to a prior discussion on "flatness" that he had with Charles [research assistant]. This occurred to him after he left last time, but he did not think of it consciously, he felt, when drawing; yet he felt it influenced him while drawing. The idea was to outline arm, boots, etc., and more or less disengage them from the rest of the forms, abstractly or flatly, to show the idea through significant parts.

Today he started to draw a vase, but it changed to an owl. He is studying and measuring it out studiously, using a paper towel as a measuring and line-up device.

Example 2, Frank _____, W-9, November 26, 1969; psychologist.

Frank reviewed his last week's production, a man climbing steps, leaning into a rain storm. Again Frank expressed dissatisfaction; he was not able to produce what he intended. Placed one smaller figure in the background, but had intended to place several other figures in the background. Tried a tree, converted it to a lamp post. Neglected face and hand. Says the boots, umbrella, and leaning into the wind are the essential elements of the idea.

Talked about a form of depictive art which is essentially flat or two-dimensional. Trying deliberately to suggest the whole by drawing a part. This idea spontaneously occurred in this drawing session and he thinks this idea may have been occurring subconsciously last week, when he made the drawing.

This will be a short session, as the viewing and discussion took some 30 minutes. Frank talked more about his work this time than at any previous session.

Again is working from imagery. "I was going to draw a vase, but now I think it will be an owl." "Wow, I don't know what it will be."

The production comes slowly, with much reflection. Figure only partially outlined, but spending a great deal of time on the outline and the little detail included. Concluded 3:30. Not completed.

Example 3, Frank _____, W-9, November 26, 1969; C.C.S. [research assistant]

Some weeks I am silent. Other weeks the words just pour out. This week I pushed Frank (in the inquiry) harder than most times. I run the risk of forcing him into corners, and even worse my corner. He had *idea* to draw a windy day. It was that way last week. Drew a stick figure first and then filled in. Didn't look right. Put in the steps (reminded him of library steps). Drew lamp post and tree to fill in, but didn't like them and erased both. Second figure on the right just a fill-in, like shark figure earlier.

He would have filled in the background if he had a model. Not well pleased with position of umbrella. Would have preferred it lower to emphasize the *idea*.

I asked if he meant feeling compared with form. "Form?" "Shapes, yes, I understand." (Didn't seem to think of this separation of idea and form.) I mentioned the skull (W-5) as more concerned with form?

He knew the hands weren't complete, but they weren't needed in this drawing. He just can't do them, either—maybe if he had a model, he said.

Started to draw a vase. Stopped, turned to us and told us it was an owl.

I pushed this week but John is now in our groove. Seemed interested and attentive to all I said. Wanted to help us, and *now maybe himself. Now maybe himself*—happened once or twice last week, but *NM himself* was impossible in the first month, I think.

Several things make the notes presented above different from straight T-data. To begin with, some of the events we record are transmitted to us via Frank's first-person-singular statements concerning how he made his drawing, as these are stimulated by the process recall and our questions. Second, we inquire about past events in the context of the present drawing. Third, to varying degrees we intrude our evaluations and insights as interested persons, as well as neutral observers (see especially example 3 above). The notes, in a sense, represent our own effort as scribes and historians to record, recall, and connect what is memorable, and to put it in a form befitting our perceptions.

Even so, the notes are an abstraction and selection out of highlights from the inquiry under stimulated process recall, plus observations in the context of the lab of the drawings being formed, and from comments made by the artist drawing and after current drawings. In contrast to the lab notes, the inquiry sessions themselves are taped and transcribed verbatim. These give as faithful an indication of what transpired as words alone can do, for here there are no selections or deletions or recastings into different words or our memory of them. In one sense, such transcriptions are primary evidence of what I have called an indirect representation of the artist's stream of consciousness as mediated by stimulated process recall and special participant observers. Here is an example from a session with Larry, which occurs during his second term in the drawing lab, separated by one year and one term from his first term as a participant. Figure 3 shows the three drawings to which he refers in the transcribed inquiry session. The entire session's inquiry is given verbatim. (*B* is the author, *L* is Larry, *C* is a research assistant.)

LARRY ————, WINTER 1970, W-3
1/28/70

B. Got into a bit of texture, Larry? Did you have the whole idea of the landscape in mind?

L. No, just the movement of the trees—the lacey quality. The other things I put in because I thought they were kind of funny—next to a sewer and a motel sign. The kind of things you see along the side of a road. . . . I did the trunks first, with the . . . paint is it? . . . like you said, it has a little texture in it. I didn't want it that heavy. I didn't know how it was going to work. But, that kind of look is what I wanted to do.

B. It was pretty much what you were after? You say it got a little heavier than you wanted it to up there?

L. Yeah. I wanted it to be a little thinner.

B. Did you do those more quickly than the other lines?

L. Yeah, I guess I did. I knew I wanted to get a certain look, a certain openness. It would have been a lot better if those lines had been thinner. I thought I could get it with quick brush strokes but I guess I was applying too much pressure on the brush.

B. The pressure went along with the thickness.

L. Yeah.

B. The quickness—did it have to do with the feeling of growing too?

L. Mmm—I was . . . I figured that I just wanted to get a kind of lacey effect, the kind of thing on the trees when it's real cold and they just—I just didn't care too much about placing them very carefully.

B. It was the effect you wanted, not the details.

L. Yeah. I thought I could do it that way . . . there it's just more fleshed out. I don't know that I was doing anything new there.

B. Did you have in mind their going back along the road?

L. It was kind of like up over a bank. Against the gray sky with the black trees—it's kind of an interesting thing when you're driving along.

B. As far as your original idea, did it seem to need anything more at this point [before sewer, sign, etc.]?

L. No, I don't think so.

B. It was at this point that you decided to add more?

L. Yeah. I decided to put something in with it. I put in the top of a sewer—a drainage ditch, and outlet or something. It's the kind of thing you see along the road, kind of strange.

B. Strange juxtaposition.

L. Yeah. I just put it there in kind of a fun way. I just kind of liked it—but I didn't
think it was that important. Then I put in that sign, and the road. The road
wasn't anything. The sign was just another funny kind of thing you see along the
road. The motel sign . . . the line along the side of the road—I used some gray.
It kind of had a nice feel to put it on like that.

B. A very direct way.

L. Yeah. I don't really like the rest of the stuff I put on.

B. Some more shading?

L. Right.

B. How do you feel about the first one you did?

L. It's o.k. I kind of chuckle.

C. Is it the first time you've used that ⌈paint⌉?

L. The acryllic—yeah. I like using it. It's a lot nicer to work with.

B. You prefer that to the ink and charcoal, etc.?

L. Yeah. It makes kind of a feel . . . oh, these are the boxes.

B. This is the one you did in one of your notebook sketches.

L. Right there is where I ran into trouble . . . the three ⌈boxes⌉. It was grounded
right away. It ran off the page in kind of a bad way. Not like the other one I did.
That was like the foundation—it had a strong foundation. Anything I put on to
it didn't seem to shake it—it didn't make it.

B. The relationship wasn't right for you?

L. Once I did that I couldn't . . .

Figure 3.   Larry's drawings

B. Did you know what was wrong there?

L. If I . . . had started up in the left-hand corner more, I maybe could have worked it down, kind of a straggling kind of effect . . . kind of built them down, instead of having them look like it was setting there . . . I wanted to have them look like they were tumbling or something.

B. It became too solid.

L. It was like I put a foundation on it and from there it could take anything I put onto it, at least in my eyes anyway.

B. The idea you had before showed it kind of like tumbling?

L. Kind of . . . kind of, you know, weak . . . the way they were set, they didn't look good. They looked like kind of a ramshackle house . . . it didn't *look* like a ramshackle house, but as kind of opposed to a solid brick house . . . like an old wooden shack that was half crushed in . . . kind of bent out of shape.

B. These got too solid?

L. Yeah.

C. When did that happen, do you know?

L. I think it was up in the left there. There when I put in that third block [at this time the negatives are being rerun]. I think if I had started those other two up in the left further and worked it down somehow. Like . . . go on to the next one; I think it'll show it. I got that one up in the corner, the top one, the highest one . . . if you just look at those three, from those on anything I put in was . . . you see those three were so solid that all the other things I put on just hung on to them.

B. You tried to treat these next ones a little more loosely you said.

L. Yeah. I tried to get them to shake it up a bit.

C. It looks like they don't belong, the others are so solid.

L. The other ones are . . . you know, abominated.

B. It looks like you got some granite in with your cardboard so to speak.

L. Yeah. Too much structural steel in the darn things. They'll never crumble.

C. How do you feel about those other three—not the first three, but the other three.

L. They're kind of interesting. They aren't exactly what I was trying to do. I was trying to get an effect with more strongly shaped boxes. Those are kind of a different way of getting at it.

C. They're looser, but in another sense they're not boxes either. They're contorted and twisted.

L. Trying to make the angles in there, they're not really rectangular.

C. The first three are solid, but the problem is that they had a foundation. The others have less of a foundation, but then they don't become solid.

L. Yeah, they're broken up, and I tried when I started out to use more solid figures, but do so just by their positioning, by their relationship to each other they'd be looser.

L. [new picture] That's the Ebervale Post Office. That's what it is.

B. Is that an actual place.

L. Yeah. Last summer, I worked outside Ebervale, surveying. We went in there a couple of times for a soda after work.

B. A little store in there?

L. Yeah, a little store, and the door covered about as much of the front space as I've showed it there, and the grays are what I tried to get because it's kind of a gray. It's attached to a bigger building at the left which turned out to be a bar, to the left, the Valiant Bar, to the left—a bigger more strong building. This is kind of tacked on. It's old. The inside is really interesting. It's got a scale that hangs—a spring scale with a big brass bucket that they put the tomatoes or cold meat in. And behind it an old type of glass-front candy counter.

C. Where is this?

L. Outside of Hazleton. To the right as you go in they have the post office part—very little, with a little window, all the wanted posters on a little clipboard, and all these wooden pigeon holes where people come for their mail. And there's an old guy that seems as though he was built along with the place. And it seems as though they'll both probably die at the same time.

C. He was sleeping over in the corner of the general store and one day they built a post office around him.

L. Yeah, and there's an old Coke machine on the right side. It's an ice box—no refrigeration. It's rusty, square, dumpy. It's a nice place.

C. But you wouldn't want to live there.

L. No. There's one wire going into it. No refrigeration, just enough power for a light. . . . As you look at it, I guess it's on the lower side of the road, on the bank, you look at it and get the perspective that I'm looking at it. And of course there are all coal banks behind it in the distance . . . strip mining, and the shale and stuff on top; but in the distance you can see that behind it . . . all black hills, mountainous things deposited by big steam shovels.

B. And they have some really big ones too.

L. Some of the world's biggest—two of the biggest. The road runs from Hazelton to Freeland. Hazelton's pretty small and Freeland's smaller yet. Ebervale's about, maybe, 20 houses. I don't even know if there are that many. Along the left side of the road—behind Ebervale—there's a vein of coal, back about a quarter mile. There's an old company town, put up by the old coal barons. Kind of an interesting thing. The standard of living's . . . you're kind of well off if you've got this new asbestos siding on your house, over the old wood. This is old wood. Of course it's painted. It's gray. It's old and dirty and stuff, but at least it's covered. A lot of the others aren't. I'm kind of the Chamber of Commerce of Ebervale. . . . That [on the slide] is the edge of the next building [the bar]. Maybe it used to be a hotel, two stories high.

B. This is the part of the country you come from?

L. Yeah. I live in Hazelton. [on slide] I'm putting some more of the black on there. I didn't bring it down to the roof. I don't know why. I just thought it looked better that way.

B. Just left a space there?

L. Yeah. I thought it gave it distance there.

B. You didn't plan originally to bring it down?

L. No. I started up high and I just didn't bring it down. I just kind of outlined the roof, but I kept it about an inch or so out. It looked pretty good like that to me.

B. It brought more emphasis to the house, like?

L. Yeah. I think if I'd have brought it right down it would have closed in on the building. . . . Like I didn't try to get too much dimension. It was kind of like a flatter type of thing.

B. You wanted it flat?

L. Yeah.

B. Did that flatness have anything to do with the grayness? Simplicity . . . and all that.

C. One-dimensional thinking . . .

L. I don't know. I think the first thing I did in the picture . . . yeah, I remember now . . . I put the window up on the top there. I don't know why. Maybe I wasn't quite sure I was going to do that picture. I just kind of [makes "one, two, three" noise and gesture]. And everything kind of went around it from there. . . . Anyway, I kind of like the looks of it. It has all the things I really ever wanted to show about the Ebervale Post Office. I didn't think about bringing the eaves out, or trying to make the door look like it has a step . . . and the mountain there . . .

B. It all goes with the feeling of the Ebervale Post Office.

L. I'm not exactly sure. I don't know if it's all that way, or just kind of the feeling I got that day . . . kind of the image in my mind. I'm kind of satisfied.

B. Does this one work more for you than the first one?

L. They're like two different things.

B. Not comparable?

L. No. I was concerned with a different kind of thing, kind of an image of a feeling. Over there, with the trees, it was more of a visual thing. The branches, in the winter, are so stark, it's such a powerful, striking thing. I just wanted to try to get that. And after I did that I just added things like you might see . . . scraps . . .

B. On the negatives, the trees seemed almost complete in themselves, but you wanted to show the contrast—the way you experience these things. These are a part of the environment too—the way you come upon it. The third one is more a problem in characterization, was it?

L. Yeah, that was something more that just stuck upon me. Like I said, the mood way . . . I was doodling and all of a sudden there was something there.

B. The image wasn't there at the start.

L. No.

C. Actually, you started out with a square, almost like the second one. It might have had a relationship to the squares, but you didn't want to follow it?

L. I don't know. I remember now, when I first did that, no. 2, maybe I was just doing flat stuff.

B. That interests you, the idea of showing something flat like that?

L. Yeah. If I did more of them, I might get some idea of what I was doing and why.

B. Do you think these coal mountains had any relationship to making it flat.

L. I put those in that way to keep them back. They weren't supposed to have any dimension. Kind of a flat behind flat.

B. That's what I meant.

The above transcription shows some of the subtle interactions between the special participant observers and the artist. It is not my intent to discuss these here. Rather, I have wished to give an example of verbal material, indirect and direct, but the one not completely separable from the other, which acknowledges three things: the need for the artist's first-person-singular statements concerning his work as stimulated toward recall of process; the need for special participant observers whose role is toward appreciation and understanding; and the admission that as special participant observers we are a part of the artist's drawing series, even if in an indirect way (that is, in a way claiming no causal relationship between our reflections with the artist and what he subsequently does). It is important that our entry into the artistic serial in no way usurp artistic causality, idiosyncratic meaning, and intentional symbolization on the artist's part.

First-person-singular Narrative

None of the examples presented under the various alternative modes discussed in this book is purely fictional. Each is based on sources of evidence and information like those listed above under mute evidence, lab notes, and transcriptions of inquiry sessions. In this section we will explore the kind of insight possible through the imaginative effort to rewrite the available information on a drawing's evolution as though the artist were thinking to himself as he works.

Of course just what that thinking is like neither the artist nor our accumulated information can tell us with certainty. Hence I refer to this effort as one of imaginative reconstruction in the subjective or stream-of-consciousness mode.

Several years ago, my research assistant, a visiting psychologist, and I each tried, one at a time with no one else present, to verbalize as naturally as possible as we drew. We concluded that the process was unnatural, interfering with the ongoing drawing. Even so, my curiosity impelled me to go back and listen to the tape I had made while drawing. I was working on a tree series motif. It seemed to me that verbalizing strongly affected what I did. The associational chain of words seemed to make my drawings string out, usually unfinished, from one exploration to another. Purely aesthetic considerations (whatever they might be), as less verbalizable aspects of drawing, yielded to verbalizable goals or criteria suitable for evaluation under the guidance of my feelings of emerging qualities of the work. Here is an excerpt about half way through the tape:

Working wet on wet is not completely the way I want it. . . . Better now. Can't be too wet. . . . Hmm. Having trouble here with the ink. Something I'll have to play with more. What I'm after is some way to suggest the feeling I got when I saw the pattern on the road . . . of tree branches in the moonlight. That pattern is relatively vague . . . and random. But vague and random in a curious way. Again, I guess I'm thinking of a possible pottery decoration, but don't need to. . . . Scrubbing around a bit helps there. In this case it's just the opposite from the lacey trees. Probably how to get a feeling of definiteness without being definite . . . and a clear pattern without having a clear pattern visible. I find it hard to verbalize. In this case it shouldn't be recognizable to any great extent. [Inaudible statement.] Working without design requires more. [Inaudible statement.] . . . I seem to be working more on effects of wet. I don't know what to say . . . of course you could reason you're now getting more into the effects of water and so forth . . . that doesn't work. . . . Nothing it helps to verbalize. Verbalization places me on a different plane of abstraction . . . mostly. . . . It's getting some of that quality now . . . of holding on to that pattern, but being quite elusive, simultaneously. . . . Its structure is almost root-like in its tangle. [Inaudible statement.] And I felt it . . . out of nature . . . out of a walk. The running water has something in common with it, because it flows . . . and the light flows. . . . Well . . . for what that's worth. I'm not completely succeeding. It still helps to objectify it, anyway, medium is appropriate in a way. It might be in the case of the [inaudible] tree shapes . . . the brush might do better in establishing the general flow. I'll try just a few branches . . . I goofed a bit . . . I think it does work . . . a little heavy-handed . . . but there's something in the general feel I like . . .

Perhaps this just indicates that I'm quite verbal, at least under a first attempt at talking aloud while working. The ellipses in the transcription indicate pauses. Maybe if I did this more, the pauses would be longer, because I would not feel the need to speak all the time. The inaudible areas of this short transcription suggest that some of the speaking is close to "inner speech" and not articulated clearly enough even for a sensitive microphone.

I present this material first, because it gives one slant on the unanswerable question concerning what form first-person narrative reconstructions should take. The direct "authorship" of acts and the indirect authorship imaginatively reconstructing the authorship of acts are different affairs. We draw a drawing, possibly accompanying it with rudiments of inner speech. We do not talk a drawing accompanying it with only rudiments of drawing. It is what might be called inner drawing, actual drawing, inner speech and transformational, analogical, and evaluative thinking linked with drawing that are our concern. It has been assumed that purely external perspectives on drawing desensitize us, making us forget that each drawing is a unique series of acts taking place within one person's drawing serial, in a definite time and place. We can attempt to "come near" to its reality as a psychic event by moving as close to the "authorship consciousness" as possible, via our role as special participant observers.

Let us look at an example of reconstruction in the first-person-singular mode. The example given is that of a college undergraduate who has returned to the drawing lab for a third term (ten weeks). He had first come in fall 1968, then returned in winter 1970, and in this example has just begun the spring 1970 term. The information upon which this reconstruction is built is a transcription of a feedback inquiry, but in this instance the stimulated recall is immediately after the drawing was made and is via a videotape replay of the entire drawing. I have chosen this instance in the belief that more of the authorship feeling might arise in this setting than where the recall is delayed and where it is stimulated by time-lapse photographs only. (Interestingly, this student discusses his preference for delayed recall via the time-lapse photographs on the same transcription from which I draw my information. In his view, the delayed recall is more helpful: "I like the idea of painting and going away from it, not saying too much. Turn the engine off and let it spin. . . . The only thing I'm concerned about is that the T.V. doesn't hinder a kind of thoughtful, emotional reflection after doing it . . . a kind of soul-searching 'how did it work?' 'How could I have done it otherwise?' . . . This way might be recall only. I don't say anything on my own. The other way, maybe things just kind of jell. . . . It's easier this way. I *can* come out with some fresh things about when I was working." The last statement suggests the

appropriateness of the immediate recall via videotape for the present purpose.)
Figure 4 reproduces the drawing which the example below attempts to relive
from a subjective angle.

Let's see . . . I'd like to try to get that bad downtown Baltimore feeling. I
can see it. How to begin? Like I'm right in the middle, everything stronger than me.
But how to get it on the page? What lines to hang it on? They need to fan out like.
Guess I'll just jump in. Stronger, bolder strokes. There . . .

Figure 4. Larry's Baltimore scene

Better watch how I mix the black and white paints. I'll lose that grungieness of outdoors against that black, black inside feeling—the bar, the strip show. The black's gotta count . . .

Those bars are darker than anything I've ever seen. Evil . . . terrifying! Maybe with some sticky white paint here . . . thick. Laid on. But what's a white sidewalk doing in Baltimore? Dirty it up a bit.

Now what to do? The angle's not quite right. Seems I'm up above it, damn it. I just can't handle the technical stuff. Let's get what it'll do anyway. That paint mixing is helping. Maybe if I used different brushes for each different color and changed them, three different shades . . . black, white, grays. I'll give it a little touch of white. Maybe if I draw this outside doorway here, just to highlight it with a little bit of white . . . not so's it's noticeable, but it just kind of works on the eye in an unconscious way.

Let's take a look. Geeze, that looks impressionistic almost. Didn't mean it to. Really want to be more literal.

That bar door really struck me. Don't want to pin it down but it's gotta be there, it's for real. How to get the right strokes and the feeling. They gotta catch the shapes. Well, it's better than when I started painting. . . . Trying to paint it gets you more aware. Like that dumb-ass feeling about the grass on the Hub this morning—really green, and the shapes in it. Baltimore's just the opposite. Those forms were too much for me. Only broken-down whores and bums that drink. What were they drinking? Adrura port, or something like that. Broken-down people. Broken-down town. That's all you see . . .

There . . . a billboard beside the bar. Don't have to see it too clear. "Naked show." And another black door. It wasn't really. But everything you walked into was black. . . . Surrounded by darkness.

Now, these grays. . . . Wait, they don't go with the rest of the picture. Break it up a bit.

Take another look. What should go up there in the left? I don't know what would bring it together.

Just some building above the bar. First floor, second floor—I don't know what's up above. But . . . from the ground up it's dingy. Not too much definition. Just surrounding walls. The blackness, the dinginess. . . . That's the whole thing. Smog in the sky. Don't even have to look up, it's there. It's *on* you.

This sure sharpens you up. You have to get right to it . . . face to face with a visual problem. Can't just be some vague, undefined thoughts. Don't know what I'm really doing when I'm drawing, but I've gotta be more aware of my feelings, perceptions.

There, a window . . . kind of. Don't know what I had in mind. A big, old window. Kind of interesting like that, on the second floor. All over the place and all different. Maybe it'll tie things together some.

Here below . . . the eye-catching stuff. Then those other vaguer things on top.

Now, some marks on this section. Those dash marks . . . works somehow. Don't know what it suggests. Kind of impressionistic. Need some different shape in there. Maybe like an old brownstone. The buildings are all different. Different, but no clean detail. There, with the bigger brush. Hey, I can lay these different brushes on each other. White window shade with this, some jabs of black here, mixes right on the page. Beats one brush, like before.

Whoops, too runny there on that door. I'll wipe it off with some towel. There. That scrap paper helps me keep it not too runny, not too heavy.

Better study it now. Want it to be consistent. Not too literal.

That white paper there's disturbing. Some white and gray on it. Now, touch it up a bit. Geeze, it looks too impressionistic. Still, it'll be too broken up if I get too definite. Let it flow a little vague. Those empty spaces still bother me. And a little more black on the window . . . that blackness underneath the shades. Just like in the bar. Hmm . . . white paper changes with even white paint on it. Works better.

The blackness inside is the controlling type thing. Hard with just three colors. Maybe with more I could concentrate on using the blacks here and here and here . . . make them stand out more.

There. There's a lot I can't do like I want. But it *is* Baltimore mood.

In rereading this example, and even comparing it with my own earlier effort at verbalizing when drawing, it occurs to me that the narrative could be tied more

closely to drawing acts than I made it. To give the reader a different flavor, therefore, I am including another example. This one concerns a drawing by the same
young man, this time from his first term in the drawing laboratory. The reconstruction was done by Steele.[4] Figure 5 reproduces the drawing in question.

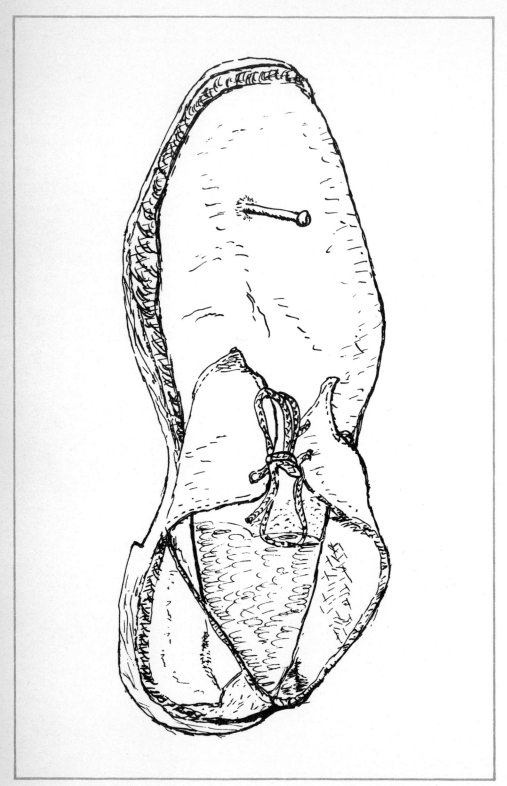

Figure 5. Larry's drawing of old shoe.

Let's see, maybe I'll try that old shoe . . . that's it—down to here. No, a little longer. O.K. Now it looks like the toe part. Hmm, let's see—I wonder how you are supposed to show leather. Well, I can see right away I'm having trouble. I don't know how to master the technique for the shadow in the leather. I can see right— I can't make the smooth that, ah—it's so flat. Well, that's feeble! Maybe like the ball—like this—it would have been a lot better if those lines were thinner. Guess it was too much pressure with the hand. Putting in a second figure here for the shadow —that seems reasonable. That's not as stubby—guess some more.

How would you indicate light—how do they want to indicate light with black pen lines? Here in the sense from this angle, maybe don't see a distinct line. Here again I can't produce what's out there. Maybe I should have tried the chair. It has simpler lines—try with less ink to modify this line a little bit to indicate a small mound. That's not what I wanted. There again I wish I knew the technique to that high spot on the paper. Maybe just a broken line along here—that's more what I wanted.

I wish I could capture some of that old shoe look.

One of the problems I sense in first-person narrative reconstructions is a kind of reductionism unavoidable even here. Perhaps repeated efforts would make me more sensitive. In trying to relive a drawing, from inside as it were, the serial prespective is broken, and we may end up with what is directly action-related and what is easily verbalizable or sharable. For example, I cannot transmit any of the sense of wonder and mystery that made that tree branch tangle pattern in the moonlight on the dirt road so memorable to me that I wanted to try for it again —in a pottery decoration with a sensitive brush held on the end of a three-foot pole, or in the wet on wet ink exploration of the transcription. In like manner, the artist's feeling about downtown Baltimore, when he went there for a physical examination prior to induction into the army, and how all of this fit into his life problems and projections, is not communicated by too close a hold on one drawing process. Such efforts as these can conceal as well as reveal. "Tell all," someone has said, "but not the song the Sirens sing"; lest, I suppose, one would not believe it himself. Seen only as a mode, that is, apart from some larger purpose, such verbalizations, too, can be reductive.

I had to choose, however, between the possibility of distortion and reduction on the one hand, and giving no examples on the other. I have chosen to risk examples, through so doing renders me vulnerable. It is my hope that, poor as they may be, they will offer a less pale, more human shadow than current circumlocutions in our literature. The probable solution to this problem lies in the more full-blown artistic serial history where this mode is only one of a number of presentational and interpretative devices, and where the problem of what the knowledge is for becomes a conscious issue.

The Multiple-consciousness Narrative

In the sketchy examples above, it is obvious that we are not really limited to the artist's stream-of-consciousness but rather deal with some representation of it further removed from it. Even when I mumbled aloud into a microphone as I drew, this was so, for I responded to my own verbal feedback, and one of the difficulties I encountered was how to counteract the string of verbal associations occurring *above* my drawing, as it were, and not *in* it. So even in this case multiple viewpoints were engaged.

Here, however, we wish to explore briefly the possible advantages of consciously extending viewpoints. In the information I draw upon for my reconstructions, I, my assistant, the drawing studio, and the like, are all ingredients, in addition to the artist's direct drawing processes and those same processes as we can indirectly approach them. We have, in short, multiple consciousnesses at work and in interaction already. We only need to tease them out and intertwine them freely for the richest reconstruction possible.

An interesting side issue appears. Were I a literary artist, perhaps I would do as well, or better, unhampered by the search for a tangible base of information upon which to erect my reconstruction. My spontaneous insights, my imaginative immersion in the artist's active person, and the like, might carry more conviction and feeling of truth as a literary projection than the more passive historical desire to probe, amass evidence, and reconstruct. This I must admit, and with it the likelihood that my low ability in the modes discussed so far is a function of my combined desire to understand and appreciate on the one hand, and to ameliorate the condition of that which I study, in addition to achieving a kind of knowledge (or nonabstract theory), on the other. In short, I cannot give you good literature. I aspire more to give you good psychology and good art education. (And, of course, even in the latter two cases, I would have to add "of a particular kind.")

The example which follows, however, is a simple descriptive narrative, utilizing material from various points of view. It is presented from my point of view (at least that is what the "I" implies). I have changed the names of the artist, the visiting psychologist, and my assistant. The three drawings mentioned in the example are shown in chronological order in figure 6.

Figure 6. Frank's drawings

Dr. Hamlin from Psychology came to the drawing lab for the first time today, to watch Frank drawing. I was a little uneasy, not knowing how Frank might react to a new observer, and may have projected that. Bill, my assistant, was out. I fumbled about trying to get the negatives in the filmstrip projector the right way. Finally, the image was on the wall of the darkened room. Bill came in just after the series of negatives started. He greeted Dr. Hamlin. They had a little chitchat while we got resettled, and I went to my preferred place, on the bench, between Frank (on the drawing stool) and the white celotex wall where we projected the negatives. Bill took over the projector.

Last week Frank had brought in an oak leaf to draw. The idea to do so was suggested to him by what an art major friend had to do for a class project, he told us. His friend had started with pine needles, but she went back to a leaf too.

When I took the time-lapse photos last week I observed the stages of Frank's drawing through the little window behind which the camera is mounted out of sight. (The photographs are taken from a front-surface mirror mounted over Frank's drawing board on a forty-degree-angle.) I was frankly surprised by Frank's skills in rendering the oak leaf. His first drawings (the first two weeks) were quite primitive, compared to the realism of the leaf. He was able to modulate the light and shade, show variations in contour and contour shading—the shadow of the leaf on a flat surface. I noticed he put in the fine veins first, but they became almost indiscernible after the first shading. Frank had said that this was what he was after—a 3-D look. He was able to concentrate on the goal of depth. Two weeks ago his mind had wandered as he tried to draw the squirrel in an oak tree, from memory.

Today, with the negatives projected in order on the wall, Frank wasn't saying much. He verified again that the ribs went in first, then the outline lightly, then the details of the outline, the finer veination, some shading, and finally more shading with a softer pencil. It was hard to follow the negatives at first, because the pencil lines were so light. Frank said he didn't prefigure how he'd do the leaf, or that he'd add the shadow. I learned that the sharpest detail and veination was mostly where the light hit the leaf.

"Putting shading in on the side of the fine veination, you lose some of the detail, is that right?" I asked. Frank said it didn't concern him that the veins were mostly lost with the shading.

"How does it look after a week's lay off?" Bill asked Frank.

"O.K. I don't know," he replied.

"What's up for today?" Bill continued.

"You got me!" answered Frank.

"I didn't mean to *get* you," Bill said, trying to ease what might have seemed like pressure on Frank to produce.

Bill and I went to work, busying ourselves with chores related to the room. Dr. Hamlin seated himself, with notepad in hand, to Frank's left. In the rear, Bill and I fell into conversation about articles we were reading.

Dr. Hamlin took careful notes of what followed: Student thinks approximately 10 minutes. Thrice turned pad horizontally: marked, erased. Began to draw. Curving line—outline. Worked within outline. Erased portion of outline and retraced. Began to elaborate on outline at "top." (Took first picture after 5 minutes.)

Still working on "top" of outline. (Picture, 2 minutes.) Studying the sketch. (Picture, 2 minutes.) More detail "inside" outline. (Picture, 2 minutes.) Studying sketch—more fine detail, on lower edge—shading.

Studying sketch—working at right side—working at left side—emphasizing small detail shading work.

Ponders quite a bit—pencil work is little by little. Chin on hands. Jiggling knees on stool. Picture seems to be evolving bit by bit—out of thin air.

Working on shading bottom edge.

No clear idea of what he wishes to draw? Evolving from his behavior itself?

Head on arm; much squirming.

Pencil tapping, shading. (E's continue to talk in background.)

Pencil work at bottom of sheet.

Thinking, pondering. Not looking at sheet?

Shading behavior.

Left upper half—new outline appears.

Heavily shading this new figure.

New outline "sketched"—rather hesitantly—UL of page, line continues to right and back toward left.

(Appears to be a fish.)

Erasure.

Studying drawing. Long period of 2-3 minutes. More shading in figure at UL.

Vigorous shading.

Tapping cheek. Squirming. Erasure (pencil eraser is almost even to metal ferrule). Great deal of erasure—more than a minute. (No pencil sharpening yet.) Uses brush to clean drawing.

Shading at right. Erasure in same area. Much erasure—UL and UR (55 minutes since session began). Erasure continues. Studying the page.

Erasing? or smudging? Seems intentional smudging. Told it's 3:20 but he can work as long as he likes.

Frank decided to stop work. He was about finished anyway.

"It's a shark picture," he volunteered before leaving. "I've been dissecting a shark in anatomy class this week." After a brief pause: "I couldn't remember how many gills there were. It made me really mad at myself."

We learned that Frank had not intended to draw the other three sharks. They just came in—perhaps, he mused, because the tail of the front big shark ran off the page at the right, he brought in the tail of another on the left. Then followed other sharks, in planes of space. He got the image of them then in a murky ocean setting. "They look like ghosts in the background," he said.

He had used the blunted eraser end to smudge out the original sharp outlines. The sequence was as Dr. Hamlin recorded it, but now we had the intention behind it:

outline, detail, shading, spill-over shading (to suggest distance and water), smudging and blurring. Frank even blurred out the rock, flower and seaweed, details, and the large foreground fish to a degree, to show the water medium. He was disturbed about the open-water areas, not knowing how to represent the water itself when not on an object. "I'm sure an artist would have a way to handle it." Then, too, the picture lacked a clear demarcation between ground and water (even though a rock and flower were shown).

"I really don't know if I'm any use to you, nor what I should do—what I could do to help from your point of view," he said apologetically. We tried again to assure him we had no expectations about what he was to do and that from our point of view he was doing fine.

After Frank left, the three of us discussed Frank's method of doing an object in detail and then transforming it by some other operation—for example, the leaf veins, then shading and losing them; and the fish detail, then smudging and rubbing it out. Dr. Hamlin thought this might come from Frank's biology background. This seemed plausible enough, but later evidence failed to support this hypothesis. I found a kind of structure and charm in the thinking processes Frank seemed to be using. It reminded me of Lowenfeld's haptic blind sculptors who made the eye socket, entered in the eyeball, then put the lid over it. Even though later transformations hide much of the earlier preparatory work, a kind of honest structure is there, underneath.

Literary Psychology

Under the general heading of presentational modes we have moved from mute evidence and direct T-data to reconstructions close to the artist's subjective angle, then to many angles or many consciousnesses as they surround a unique time-space artistic process. The "otherness" that creeps in as we leave the subjective angle is intensified within the series of modes that follows it, and this will continue by and large in those taken up in the next chapter. Even, however, in the first-person-singular presentation, the hand of the writer is present. This is just as true if we try to reconstruct our own stream of consciousness. There is a reflectiveness and reflexiveness necessarily attendant upon our effort which may not so much be a flaw as an enrichment in the effect. At the most we can strive by our literary skill to render the reflective quality transparent, if that is our aim.

One of the questions unanswered in my mind has to do with how much reflective quality an artist must possess to make methods like the ones here described fruitful. I do not know, for example, to what degree they would be useful with preadolescents. I am inclined to feel that the methods might work but that the artist's ability to profit from verbal self-guidance as a result of reflective inquiry would be lesser. This, then, might result in a reduced motivation to participate in such sharing modes as described. I feel optimistic that other outcomes profitable to a child's art would appear, but this hunch must await study.

In a way, the name of the mode to be described in this section is misleading. It is a literary psychological vantage point, but it is applied to the kind of "nonabstract" theory-making mentioned in chapter 2, the aim of which is still to give us a grasp of a particular artist's expressive event, couching that within the artistic serial of which it is a part. The appearance of "psychology," however, as a term consciously used, moves us away from the novelist's spontaneity and toward the historian's reconstruction and interpretation under guidance of role and question. Since our concern is art, the problem is complicated, for we contend not only with views about how the mind operates, but also with those concerning the nature of art experience. My own dual identification, to the degree I am conscious of it, is what I will call a depth-cognitive psychology of the individual and an existential-expressive theory of art. (The last book of Langer's, *Mind*,[5] is as close as I can come to a comfortable available model.)

Steele discusses what he means by literary psychology:

> Another type of writing may be more psychologically oriented. . . . Both the novelistic and psychological styles take on a slightly different feeling than the first-person singular style because there is an obvious "othering." There is also a slightly different feeling between presenting the "othering" view as a novel or as psychology, sociology, anthropology and history, for the latter are an attempt to begin to theorize in a nonabstract particular way.[6]

The above quotation introduces a difference in emphasis and purpose in this last presentational mode. It is, in fact, a transitional mode, belonging equally with those to be introduced in the next chapter.

Rather than say, as Steele does above, that this mode is attempting "to theorize in a nonabstract particular way," one might say that the person working in this way is inclined to approach the phenomena he aims to present under the guidance of some psychological theory, the general principles of which will influence his perception and representation of the individual case. Thus a Freudian or neo-Freudian will be sensitized toward one kind of perception and interpretation, a cognitive theorist toward another. The writings of Arnheim[7] and Ehrenzweig[8] are examples from within the literature of art and art education, except that these writers, interestingly enough, rarely, if indeed ever, present a case, either with a detailed description of one of that individual's particular artistic processes or of his artistic serial of which it is a part. Lowenfeld, especially in his first book, occasionally represents the detailed history of a child's drawing or series of drawings.[9] In his descriptions, his own role in stimulation, setting of topic, and the like, is explicitly included, for it is through the impact of this external influence that meaning arises. Typically, the child's schema or basic, uninfluenced manner of representation is first established then deflections under some influence or experience are analyzed and interpreted, as, for example, being attributable to "proportions of value," "autoplastic sensations," and "self-identification" through inclusion of the self in the drawing.

Schaeffer-Simmern[10] does not quite belong under the mode here discussed, in that his approach is based on a theory of art drawn from the thought of Gustav Britsch,[11] as extrapolated into a developmental theory. But, in another way, he represents this view well, for he is more inclined to present an individual case in some longitudinal depth, and his explanatory concepts (which also become pedagogical forces) are at least quasi-psychological.

I find myself, now locked in on the integrity and continuity of individual process and serial, hard-pressed to set to the task of representing a case under the guidance of some explicit psychological theory. Some of the philosophical and psychological concepts which have influenced me and which I am conscious of are evident in the assumptions and purposes of this book. (For an indication of the history of these influences and for an example of attempted analysis and synthesis of pertinent literature, the reader is referred to *Mind and Context in the Art of Drawing*.[12]) My procedure, in actual practice, has been that of coining new terms and labels to aid my perception and description of the individual case, arriving at these neologisms as inductively as possible. Since, however, I use the new terms for more than one case, they function somewhat like principles from psychological theory. In truth, they function more usefully when I discuss the problem of representing individual cases in the abstract, or in general. When I actually speak of a given individual, the terms do not occur as readily. In this book, for example, I have spoken of "artistic causality," "idiosyncratic meaning," and "intentional symbolization." Elsewhere, I speak of "inner drawing," "forbidden techniques," "counter-intervention," "myth of self-identity," and the like.[13] These terms are first efforts to describe how I conduct myself in the drawing lab, what I perceive, and what I expect.

Sometimes I utilize broad, abstract concepts which I feel give promise of far-reaching interpretations and insights. Let me give an example of this. It has been my impression that, in addition to their technical, representational, and transformational skills in media, artists guide themselves by semiconscious artistic concepts and attitudes. In the case of an artist with limited training and drawing skills, it is somewhat easier to see how given concepts and attitudes function to transform or transcend impoverished skills toward new and desired ends.

One of the borrowed concepts I find useful is what has been called "third-order-concepts."[14] This term, in a therapeutic or interpersonal example, indicates the following level of complexity or abstractness: "Here's how I see you seeing me seeing you." The authors from whom I have borrowed this idea feel that emphasis on such thinking, on the conscious level, is the major task in psychotherapy, and that actual change or "improvement" occurs on a "fourth level" beyond the mind's conscious comprehension, a kind of transcendence which is nonetheless prepared for by the third level "work."[15] In any specific case, too much credit may be given to this conscious work of the mind, or so the depth psychologies would suggest. In the latter view, the conscious work is often set off by less conscious influences or symbols, as from dreams, free associations, expressive symbols, and the like. In the drawing serial, both forces, it would seem, are operating. Newness arrives by multiple routes, in the drawing and in the mind, so that a constant interaction occurs and the path of the serial is projected onward.

A recent case of "sudden transformation" from this point of view was an instance in the drawing lab in which the artist suddenly dropped his typical themes and problems and produced, in rapid succession, eighteen drawings in little over an hour's time. This example is too recent to reflect on adequately, however, and at this writing we do not yet have the stimulated process recall followup whereby we can indirectly share the artist's stream of consciousness on that productive occasion. Nor do I have the subsequent sessions behind me, wherein I can read the utilization of this change in the continuing serial. The artist has already said that he has "just gotten into the fun of it all," after eight weeks in the drawing lab, and he has projected his desire to draw outside the lab, on his own, and to begin a "visual diary."

I mention the above example, however, because such startling changes are certainly prepared for, and the person representing them feels constrained to interpret and reflect upon them. Such instances are not rare, though they differ endlessly in form, suddenness, and magnitude.

For our purposes here, I will use an earlier example. This one concerns Larry, in his first term in the drawing lab, and it centers on a transformation which took place in his drawings between the sixth and seventh sessions. Drawings *a* through *n* which comprise figure 7 are interspersed throughout the following example.

In his first weeks in the lab, Larry had demonstrated that he could take liberties in his drawings, as, for example, in selecting items from a still-life, where, in week 1, he changed sizes (diminished size of screen to fit it into his drawing), showed the line of a drawer not visible to him, consciously adjusted forms to the page format, and selected elements that were simple and flat. He appeared, at the start, to be a slow and careful worker, "getting used to pen and ink."

He mentioned a philosophy teacher he had at one of the branch campuses who got him interested in the philosophy of art. He had read Dewey's *Art as Experience* and Joyce's *Portrait of the Artist as a Young Man*.

From the start, Larry had trouble with textures—"They weren't just straight lines. A face might have the same problem." We learned that he was consciously trying to "translate" visual impressions into pen marks—"pen figures," as he called them.

In his second drawing session, he tried to work out ways to represent form and light, practicing first on a spherical pot, then on an old shoe from the still life. During this session, we later learned, he discovered how to control different weights of pen lines and felt these had some relation to form, light-shade, and "perspective."

In drawing the old shoe, Larry worked on the problem of texture ("what the material is") and shadow and light, which is more or less superimposed on the form and texture. He knows the relationship between these two problems is a fluid one. Light and shade, and texture are both translated into pen-and-ink language—what he calls "pen figures." He discovered that the figure for texture had to be different from that for light and shade. He also learned that how to have these interact in actual practice was a problem, causing some visual confusion.

Figure 7 (a-n). Series of Larry's drawings (pp. 46-52).

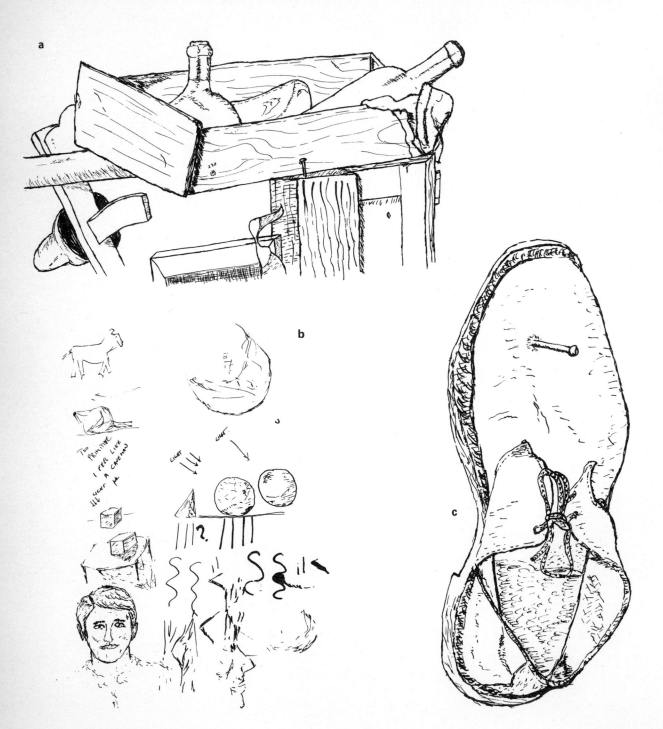

During the third session Larry worked further on his shading-light-form-texture pen-and-ink problem. He utilized a white sphere, a spherical light shade, a cube and a cylinder which were in the room (from a perception experiment). He discovered the "elliptical shadow" cast by a sphere on a plane in perspective. He transferred this discovery to the representation of a tree with spherical leaf-mass, but had trouble finding the proper elliptical shadow to stay on the plane. Here, we learned, he made an unintentional discovery which was like a minor breakthrough for him. In drawing the rough tree trunk, while working on the problem of light and shadow (interestingly, he represents the place light strikes a sphere with black pen lines, not in the classical art-school sphere-shadowing method), he unconsciously varied both weight of pen line and closeness of strokes. He then realized he was representing both texture and light-and-shade (form) at one time. This insight so excited him that he drew another trunk beside the first one, to reinforce his discovery and share it with us.

We learned that Larry's objective was to arrive at "lifelikeness," first, and "feeling" thereafter ("as in a face"). "Now," he said, "I'm like a person learning to use a hammer and saw so he can build something."

Though Larry had set himself a kind of discipline leading toward representational mastery, and though he had made some important discoveries on his own toward his goals, he seemed to be getting progressively unhappy with his work. At this same time (week 3 and 4), he saw an art exhibition of faculty work. He also drew in a sketch book away from the lab—a copy of a high-contrast Beatles photograph, a section of "Guernica," and his own pipe. He liked the spatial, in-out quality of the Beatles photograph, and responded to the freer feeling in the "Guernica" detail. He had studied the latter in art history— "It really blew my mind."

In the lab he made three drawings from a large photograph of a girl's face and shoulders (which we had hidden, but he asked for it), in Conté charcoal, and ink (he had not used the first two media before); they happened to be on the drawing table because another artist had used them just before Larry came in. Larry had admitted that it might be possible to work on his realism-mastery, technical control objective and his more distant goal of "feeling" or expression somewhat simultaneously—not wait until he had mastered "technique" and go on to "feeling."

When Larry did the photographic portrait in pen and ink, he continued his explorations and conquests from before. He began with the hair, but with no outline at the forehead; and he varied the light-shade, or value texture of the hair by *direct* pen strokes (not "by going over"). This is a departure. Lines are now very loose and open. He says he now visualizes the whole first. In this face, he put all of the hair in with some indication of ears and neck before the features. He treated all of the features but the lips with his open, no-outline strategy. He recognized that this made the lips out of context. He mentioned that he still has problems with the projection and rounding of a form. He drew a cube in perspective in miniature below the portrait, indicating how he wanted the face to thrust forward. He described a pastel face done by an art major friend. "He puts on a few strokes and smudges them in while he's putting his shirt on, and there it is. Just like I'd want it."

At this point, Larry draws W_____, a visiting art education student, from real life, in the laboratory. He was proceeding freely and liked the drawing until be added the features at the end, when he got the plane of hair and neck out of gear with the features. He was conscious of this difficulty in foreshortening (a term he did not use, however), and indicated the problem by constructing a plane of touched thumbs and extended forefingers and tilting it at different angles. After this partial failure, he did a page of quicker sketches, some from life, some schematic. Among them appear two which solve the angle of foreshortening appropriate to a head tilted downward. This was corroborated by Larry later:

Larry: If you get the lines of the forehead and chin, it's successful.
B: What does this have to do with the features?
Larry: The features still have to be placed correctly, but the right angle of the face gives a reference point.
B: [Referring to the second drawing with the quick sketches—a new technique for Larry] You didn't get hung up on details here. Was this manipulation helpful to you in any way?
Larry: I was conscious of it.
B: It's amazing how much you "read" without the features—nice quality.
W: [Who had been posing] Yes, it still catches a lot—has a nice feeling about it. Are there any particular lines to start with that make you feel right?
Larry: Yes, forehead and chin.
B: Do you feel that what you have learned about doing it will permit you to manipulate angles without the subject being there?"
Larry: Yes.
B: Are you saying that in a sense what you have to learn is not to depend on what is there?
Larry: Yes. More on not so much learning to copy exactly.

At this point, several other influences have some impact on Larry. He saw two quite dissimilar, rather avant-garde art shows. The one was that of a painting professor from the Art Department which incorporated actual projections from the canvas (as in one-half of a head, from a doll or mannikin) with more traditional painted representations. The other was a show of Flavin's utilizing only flourescent light

f

g

h

VISUAL

tubes in an otherwise darkened room. Both of these exhibitions caused him to extend still further his concept of art.

Then, during the sixth week in the lab, Larry did no drawing at all. Instead he and W_____, the art education major who had posed for him before, entered into extended discussion on a great many topics concerning (as far as I can recapture it, since I and my assistant left the two alone), W_____'s feeling about the importance of "confidence in his own thing"—whatever it seemed like. Then the talk got more abstract. Larry's ideas on literature (his major) as art are pretty clear. The talk between Larry and W_____ was quite meaningful to both.

Prior to the discussion between the two (who are essentially peers), Larry had told us of his concept of "expression," which "is the main thing in a face" and how this is different from realism. He had also experimented, on the page with quick sketches of heads, on more abstract, schematic representations. Among these was an abstract nose which Larry had consciously "flattened and formed," which still read as form and nose. He had written the word "visual" beside this, apparently to tell us of some insight, but he could not recapture that later.

The transformation in Larry's series occurred the session (week 7) after the all-talk session with W_____ (week 6). When Larry came into the lab (for week 7), he was greeted but pretty well ignored—a kind of tacit understanding that he'd draw because the session before was all talk.

Larry didn't know what he was going to draw. He focused on the broken screen of the still-life, the moiré effect of its double fold, and the shape of the whole as an abstract form. He worked out pen units to signify the light and dark pattern (using two symbols ☰☰ and #₌#). He placed these units carefully on the page. First he put in all the light units, then all the dark ones. He varied the marks in both darkness and density. He deliberately gave no setting which would identify the drawing as "screen" or "landscape" or whatever. He connected his desire to leave it open to the feeling he got at the Flavin (light) exhibition and the Montenegro (3-D and painted) exhibition. When questioned at the close of the session, Larry saw virtue in this ambiguity. It led to "interest." He also saw his approach now as under a different attitude, not bringing to bear as many rules and technical requirements before the process, and relaxing his "first the tools then the building" theory. In an interview the following week (with my research assistant, C, during my absence), further corroboration of a changed attitude occurred:

C: Was this drawing a conscious effort?

L: I did it after seeing those two displays.

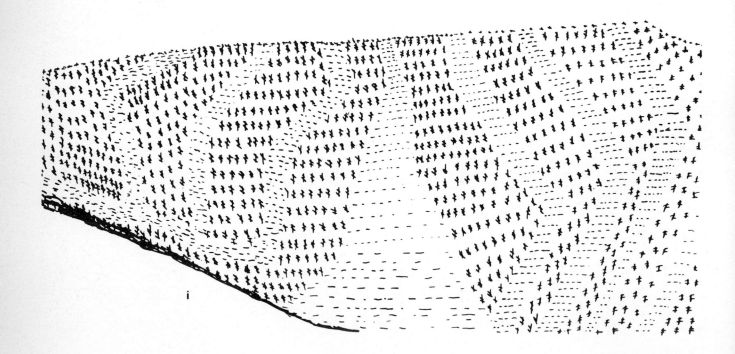

i

C: The Montenegro and the light show?

L: It's different. Before what I was building up for was so I could get realistic—make a face or something; show a mood or something like that.

C: You're implying two things: the technique and the feeling.

L: The reasoning behind it. This is different in that there's no attempt to be realistic.

Then there followed a discussion comparing literature and visual art, in which it came out that, to Larry, there could be more freedom in visual art than in literature. Larry concluded: "In this picture [of week 7] we have two distinctions. First, not being concerned so much with realism. Then we have it as a visual experience, something different."

Further corroboration of a changed view comes from an interview at the end of the term where all of Larry's drawings are put on the wall for review. He feels a "divide" happened during week 7. Before that he was "attempting realism all the time, and . . . mainly trying to get perspective and control the pen." He was also getting progressively frustrated "trying to present things realistically." The two exhibitions and his discussion with W——— kept rolling around his mind. "I guess I loosened up a bit . . . I really was tight. It was getting really depressing."

Larry further supported the interpretation that his works became more symbolic to him. As he put it: "It's more of an effect. A feeling rather than just a representation." And he acknowledged he didn't really have to know what it meant.

Subsequently, in the remaining sessions of the term (following week 7), Larry explored media much more freely, using brushes of all sizes, inventing new strokes, varying pressure, amount of water, and the like. He also developed some free "doodles," freely rearranged parts of the still life, depicting them with rapid strokes of a

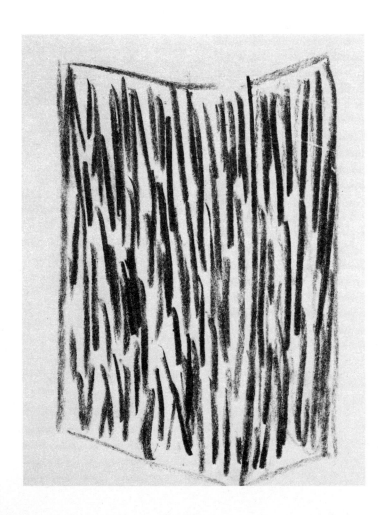

large brush; did more "abstracts" in the vein of the screen of week 7; and terminated the series with a very spontaneously rendered depiction, with a one-inch brush, of an image of a standing sculptural form (a Giacommeti "man" he had seen in the Philadelphia Museum).

Thus, in Larry's development, we see him moving from a tighter, more ego-controlled, regime of self-instruction oriented toward realistic representational skills, in which he could barely conceive of himself as interested in "feeling" or "expression," toward a relaxation of control and goal, a freer exploration of media and ideas, and a willingness to let the freedom he felt in visual art speak in its own cryptic, partly ambiguous way. There is a fuller acceptance of his limited skills (preceded by depression, even when he knew he was improving his representational ability) and a recognition of his own feelings and expressive needs. A tension develops, one might say, between the pleasure and the reality principle, but it is a healthy one with which Larry feels he can cope through exploration and daring.

The exhibitions, and the conversations with nurturant and interested others which Larry experiences, plus the reflection that stimulated process recall allows him on his own drawing methods and intentions, combine in his consciousness to produce new concepts and attitudes about art. Third-order concepts about Larry's drawing series arise from our side and his. He sees, as it were, how we see him drawing and reflecting on his drawings. And all of this is related to Larry's drawing serial. It is a part of emergent ideas, images, and methods, and he is now capable of transcending and synthesizing the cognized elements. He plays more, but he also becomes more serious. He lives more within the expressive situation itself, becoming more open to its history as unique potential for particular meaning.

n

l

m

I see, now that I have tried to present the story of Larry's change, that I am not capable of representing a single mode. At most, there is a deflection brought in by the "literary psychology" label. A rereading of the effort suggests it is neither literature nor psychology, nor an organic blend of the two. To begin with, the "facts" of the case must be established, more in T-data and mute evidence form than any other. Then, unlike the effort to apply general principles to the individual case, I am inclined to attempt a truly individualizing psychology. The outcome is more that of a psychological history of one person's drawing serial than it is that of literary psychology. I let the mode stand as it is, however, for others may be able to master what I cannot, or have no desire to. My task seems rather to reconstruct the psychic lawfulness of an individual's drawing serial from its more or less superficial empirical parts (observable, shared, and otherwise inferred). Perhaps this is what Steele really means when he speaks of "theorizing in a nonabstract particular way." I want to reveal, through what Schopenhauer calls the "empirical" (experienced or observed) character, the "intelligible" (partially inborn, partially potential, partially unrealizable) character of a unique being's artistic path, as this is seen as an aspect of his total intelligible character.[16] With the best of evidence at hand, this is perforce an imaginative representation, the end of which is an appreciation and understanding of an individuating force through the forms through which it unfolds. This is why any play with modes is at best didactic, and at worst deceptive.

Still, the modes presented in this chapter do cohere in their presentational emphasis and in their paucity of interpretation. Their expressive or literary quality must be a function of the mind and hand forming them. I invite the admittedly needed improved versions which these scant examples call forth.

Historical and Interpretive Modes Twice Removed from the Artist's Stream of Consciousness

4

Further Philosophical Considerations Relating to Modes of Inquiry into Expressive Acts

The title of this book is misleading, since I have come to insights, to expression I had not intended. What I wish for is not alternatives in a neutral world, where one damn method is as good as another; nor do I wish for a cluster of alternatives I can put in a balancing scale or huckster as superior. The Roshomon effect I alluded to earlier does have the positive aim of extensionalizing points of view concerning the expressive situation, but it also indicates that *all* points of view miss *the* point of expression. The hope was that we would come to the inexhaustible, infinite notion of expression by converging on the *presence* of the expressive transaction itself, on its very I-thou character which transcends viewpoints. At best, the clustering of finite and dead alternative extensionalizations would prepare the conceptual grounds for the illimitable, transcendent nature of each expressive movement.

For this effort not to go astray, I have maintained that we need the indirect witness of the artist who lived that expressive movement. We need, that is, closeness to the stream of consciousness that was immersed in expressing. But this is impossible, for reflecting and expressing are opposed movements. We have therefore proposed a means by which the history of events can be recalled meaningfully to the artist. Stimulated recall via process samples, however, is essentially a technique. We have added to that a relationship role, that of a special participant observer. This observer does not just gain rapport—he responds to the very otherness of the other, not only as artist, but as a thou confronting an I. The reality of expression in art as a cognition beyond comprehension is engendered by one in the other within the human dialogue. The latter, as Levinas contends in his conceptualization of the "face-to-face," is expression, transcendent, impossible of containment in encompassing thought or as a part or function of some totality.[1] Thus we have one dialogue ostensibly taking another as its subject. In the human "face-to-face" we accept and resurrect, that is, that other presence, the face-to-face which is the act of expressing in art.

Perhaps the "face" which the artist confronts in the artistic dialogue is actually his own. But this is not meant as a mirror reflection, which grimaces when he grimaces or smiles when he smiles. That would be no dialogue. This is no face-to-face. This is not "expression," again as Levinas means it, coming from "the other" toward "the same."[2] The thrust of intention from the artist is overcome by the swell of meaning rolling back from the project of expression itself.

Nor am I happy with Yeats' concept of the mask, according to which the artist plays at a self, an artistic self, "an other" than the ordinary self and one which changes in each act of expression.[3] The mask conjures up too dead an image. The "face" concept is far more potent—a living physiognomy, implicit with and overflowing meaning. It is, again to lean on Levinas, who at this point speaks most clearly toward a philosophy befitting an art education dynamically and humanly conceived, this very "exteriority," this "otherness," toward which we move from our essential and necessary base in subjectivism and separateness.[4] This otherness is the source of both the ethical and the expressive. *I* do not *express myself*. I come to a transaction, an encounter, a dialogue, in which I am overcome, transcended, in the face-to-face where expression occurs. (Levinas, it should be confessed, speaks in a timely and detailed way much as Buber did for me almost two decades ago.) Further, expression then is no satisfaction or fulfillment of my *need*. It is not taking "the other" and assimilating it to "the same." It is the movement out from a *desire* that exceeds all need and that is insatiable.[5]

Dewey speaks of the subtlety and fragility of expression in art,[6] wherein the artist must take from what is common and shared and "work" it toward what is personal and subjective (a construction similar to Piaget's synthesis of "the expression of ego" and "submission to reality" in the art of the developing child[7]). But the balance (or perhaps the imbalance should really be opposite, or toward exteriority, if anything) is somewhat destroyed in these formulations, although they do conjure up the image of the "hero" who moves out into a courageous encounter. I believe the concepts discussed from Yeats, Dewey, Piaget, and others merely reaffirm the idiosyncratic, subjective base, the nearly absolute *separation* of the self, the I, the same, out of which proceeds the transcendent, the insatiable desire for the other.

The mystical dimension which eludes my own efforts in such discussions, resides in the fact that the "self," taken in a depth psychological view, contains "the other," at least in the infinitude of potential expansions we dimly sense in our own internal life. I will term this mystical dimension more akin to Levinas's insatiable desire for the other (which by extension is that for life itself). What I have called the myth of self-identity, a myth which artistic experience promotes, but which in the fashion of true myths never solves or satisfies itself, is a symbol for the infinity of transcendences which is signified implicitly in the depth view of the self. My "works" are dead, but when a fellow human being faces *me* and we together consider these works, they signify a path, a series of events almost freed from historical time; they signify, if I may be allowed an older expression, my soul's thirst— an insatiable one for meaning and for enlargement of the self through genuine dialogue with the non-self, for an ethic of relationship and a life without fear. This is indeed what we want from all otherness. It is a relationship beyond instrumentality and will, what Levinas aptly calls a nonallergic relation to the other.[8]

This leads to a distinction between idiographic lawfulness, or between the principles proper to a study of intrapsychic relationships, and the "account" of an individual's artistic serial. The former perspective leads one in the direction of an historical determinism within the single personality. Traditionally this view is opposed to the nomothetic approach, where one discusses principles wherein all (or some) men are alike.[9] But this is not the oppositional continuum upon which I would like this book to be judged. The historical-deterministic approach, whether idiographically or nomothetically oriented, should be opposed to an approach which is nondeterministic and largely ahistorical. I have qualified the latter to a degree because there is a special kind of historical flavor to the artistic serial and to the expressive act itself. But in treating art and expression as ultimate or primitive terms, they are no longer converted into objects to be explained or analyzed from the view of a system which assigns them a subordinate place in terms of its own totality. My position is closer to Allport's, which is that events, considered in terms of the individual, and, I would add, within an existential or experiential frame of reference, are ahistorical, cutting across patterns of a lineal time stream.[10] The artistic serial (alluded to in chap. 3) seen as proactive (not reactive), as superstatic (not homeostatic), as a movement of desire (and not a reduction of need), concatenates a crazy path, evokes a dream-like vision which we can interpret, if at all, only in humility and with trembling, and I have argued, only face-to-face with the artist in a relationship wherein he can evoke his own peculiarly ahistorical memory of his stream of consciousness in the expressive act.

Yet I am caught in a contradiction, for I make something of "history," but it is of an existential, projective history. It is, as I have said, seeing the future of the artistic serial as a shared history—one, moreover, which in the sharing is not explained away, is not totalized, is not accounted for, but curiously is rendered indeterministic, pluralized through extension and open reflection, and even mythologized. The final contradiction is that I also must talk about the "cases" I know from some point of view. Hence these elucidations. I must be criticized from the points of view I am developing. All criticisms placed elsewhere are irrelevant. I would like to pluralize, open up, give art back to the artist, meet the artist as my peer and as a significant other upon whom I have no designs. Without criticisms of other efforts, including my own earlier ones,[11] this is the only ethical stance toward inquiry into the making of art I can now take.

The "twist," then, I give cases should be read against this philosophic setting. I agree with Allport when he says that the researcher sooner or later is bound to put his stamp of interpretation on the case, and that he will be able to clarify the interpretation and meaning essential to his inquiry through deliberate selection of those things he deems essential.[12] In this book I argue for alternative world views and modes of inquiry which, it is hoped, will usher in a needed pluralism where now we have largely an underdimensionalized science of man based on a reductive model borrowed from the (earlier concept of the) natural sciences which disintegrates the concept and the meaning of artistic experience and the expressive act.

Earlier I cited Collingwood's concept of artistic expression as it relates to the problem of history. The artist, he says, cannot formulate his problem beforehand, because formulation can only be read as synonymous with expression in artistic creation.

> This indeed seems to be the special character of art and its peculiar importance in the life of thought. *It is the phase of that life in which the conversion from unreflective to reflective thought actually comes about.* There is therefore a history of art, but no history of artist problems, as there is a history of scientific or philosophical problems. There is only the history of artistic achievements.[13] [Emphasis added]

It would seem, then, that when in what follows I use that ambiguous term "history," I will be doing so in different ways. First, as concerns a single artist, I can talk of the history of his artistic achievements; but I must qualify even this, because "achievements" is a word usually concealing some external frame of reference, and I have argued that what is achieved is ambiguous and most closely related to the artist's own thought, close to the expressive act where the conversion from unreflective to reflective thought comes about. *This is why all inquiries traditionally made into the making of art seem nonsensical to the individual artist. Even in the occasion where he is made an individual case he cannot be generalized within the confines of any conceptual system*—at least not as long as he lives and as long as we relate to him. (And even when he is dead, we can still proliferate "interpretations" from the same base of "facts," or find others "shedding new light.") But let us face some of these problems as we introduce the various modes of this chapter. Hard as I found the examples given in the last chapter, I find those to follow still harder.

Historical Mode

In chapter 3 we presented modes once removed from the artist's stream of consciousness. In so doing, the role played by the observer's own feelings was quite important, but these feelings were not made explicit. The special participant observer, through empathy and interest, and by utilizing lab notes, transcriptions of inquiry sessions, and pictorial evidence, tried to reconstruct as faithfully as possible what the artist did and made known through shared reflection. In other words, meaning was assumed to be implicit, first within the artist's own recollections as stimulated by process recall, and secondly, by the participant observer's shared feelings within that situation of recollection. Conceptualizations reported within the modes of chapter 3 are those which arise during the inquiry dialogue itself. As such, they have the role of guiding the series within which they are situated. In this chapter, however, the special participant observer is asked to remove himself once again to a still more abstract position, that is, one which is twice removed from the artist's stream of consciousness and to develop conceptualizations on top of the materials presented in chapter 3. This is by no means easy, because now the ongoing dialogue and its referent, the creative act, are no longer immediately present for this special participant observer. He now becomes more of an analyst, a person who is reflecting and interpreting what took place in the past. It is for this reason that the modes in this chapter, by and large, can be termed historical.

What is the aim of this special kind of history? First of all, my aim is not to imprison the artist within the confines of a tight conceptual system. Twice removed I risk interpretations, but these are tentative. There is a way in which the task that is upon me is similar to the task which was upon the artist within the inquiry sessions in the drawing lab—that is, I am asked now to reflect upon the experience which I had in the drawing lab with the artist and his ongoing series, just as the artist was asked to reflect upon his own ongoing processes of expression. My effort, thus, is a humble one, just as was the artist's. I will try through reflection to stimulate my own thinking and action forward. I will not solve problems once and for all nor come up with grandiose theories that will be a sure guide for others or for myself. Nevertheless, the effort is to share in a reasonable form reflections and abstractions pertinent to a description of expressive acts. These expressive acts are chained together in the series of one concrete, specific individual, and they occur within a definite context and time line.

At this point it may be worthwhile to digress and borrow some ideas from Gendlin.[14] His focus is on experiencing and how meaning arises therefrom. The meanings which occur in experiencing are preconceptual or implicit. Perhaps an analogy to art would help at this point. The images present within our experiencing seem to be implicit with meaning although we cannot easily or directly attach symbols to them to represent their meaning. We cannot refer to our experiencing of an image without symbols and every symbol which we apply will overlay a different meaning upon the preconceptual order. The mere fact of referring to images in consciousness is, as Gendlin points out, a symbolic act.[15] He calls this method of symbolizing one of direct reference because it merely points to the feeling or the meaning implicit without conceptualizing it. At this level, experiencing could not be shared (although there may be some communicative power in the very tone or expression of reference). Conceptualization, however, does not just *refer* to what is symbolized but *represents* it. We must symbolize experiencing for it to be known, but it need not be conceptualized.

The special participant observer has the difficult task of not only conceptualizing the artist but at each point experiencing him. At the level of historical interpretation, this special observer must deal with past and present conceptual contents which represent the artist experiencing, but now at several removes. As historian, further, his own present experiencing and conceptualizations are upon him and he has the pressing burden of realizing that each set of symbols which he applies gives a different set of meanings to the events which he is conceptualizing. What results is "not whatever meaning we wish but only just this meaning, which results from the application of this set of symbols to *this* aspect of experiencing."[16]

Therefore, to operate in the historical mode I must formulate conceptualizations which represent my experiencing of an individual artist's drawing processes and drawing series as they occurred in a given time and place. Another person could not do this in the same way because he would not be guided by the implicit meanings already present in the preconceptual matrix of my own experiencing of the given series. The conceptualizations and interpretations offered should not exhaust the meanings present in the preconceptual matrix of experiencing, but at the same time they are not arbitrary, for they do symbolize that base. It would be possible for a third party to utilize the data or given material from the drawing lab without the base in experiencing, but what would eventuate would be a different kind of order. From the standpoint of the alternatives discussed thus far in this book, this other kind of order would not be acceptable because I have based my presentation on the necessity for closeness to the artist's stream of consciousness and for a special participant observer. Therefore, it is as a special historian that I come to these events. I was present at the second order, or once removed, and the third order, or twice removed. A third party dealing with these data would be operating at the fourth level, or thrice removed, and the links between the other levels would be sundered or would have to be imaginatively constructed. His history would not be wrong or false, but it would surely be a different history and it would not meet the presuppositions upon which I have based the modes herein presented. Yet there can be no doubt that patterns at this more abstract level can be teased out and may be helpful for varying types of theories and interpretations. They are not, however, the present concern.

How does one proceed at this third level, or twice removed? First of all, I would imagine that one would review the case so that all of the material is brought back into consciousness. The data base includes all of the levels discussed within chapter 3, the levels of mute evidence, the reconstructions of the artist's stream of consciousness, and the various narratives of multiple viewpoints. The reader will note that this material is in itself uneven in that sometimes it represents mere references to the experiencing, while at other times it presents various conceptualizations of that experiencing. After reviewing all of the case material, which would be akin to a type of more or less neutral description (although I realize there are difficulties with the word "neutral"), one would then proceed to a new order of conceptualizations. The questions to be directed to any given individual case need have nothing in common with questions to be directed toward other cases. What seems essential, however, is that definite questions be asked or that key concepts or rules for interpretation be advanced. At this point, then, what might be called general principles exist which will give form to what follows. The process is to penetrate to the descriptive base of events by intuition, by recall of thoughts of the artist, by evidence-sifting—in short, by any means available to the historian. The historical "work" which follows the elucidation of principles or questions is akin to the work of analysis in behavioral research and would proceed therefrom toward interpretations, conclusions, and critique.

I have described the artist as existentially free. By this I mean that he is capable of entering into each new act of expression as though it is an honest dialogue which will transcend his expectations and his plans. One of my concerns, and one which has been supported by selective reading of philosophers and psychologists, is directed toward the kinds of conceptualizations about "making art" which the artist himself constructs and shares in the inquiry sessions. What is the nature of these reflective conceptualizations of a given artist? How does he modify and extend them from one time to another? How do these conceptualizations relate to the feelings he expresses during the inquiry sessions? What changes in processes of drawing seems to occur thereafter? Such are the abstract questions which concern me at this level. I have indicated, however, that, being general, they may not be the right questions for a given case. To put this to a trial let us consider anew one or more of the passages already referred to in chapter 3.

Please note that the conceptualizations or art concepts of which I speak are not abstract concepts to be thought of apart from the individual case context and history to which they refer. They may indeed have some meaning in a more abstract, generalizable form if they appear from time to time in a number of cases, but that is left at this point for another inquiry. The test of work in this mode is not whether the interpretations are of use to the artist but whether they do in fact add to our insight into and our appreciation of the inexhaustible meanings implicit within art experiencing. (Perhaps I can explain further what I mean by using a personal example. As a master's paper, a student has recently done a biographical sketch of my own work in pottery.[17] As she accumulated the material, transcribed interviews with me and with those who had worked with me, or known me or taught me, and proceeded to analysis and interpretation, she did in fact present for my own consumption points of view and abstractions which I would not have come to on my own. These, however, seem to have little if any impact on my present thinking and work as I come to new pottery experiences. The latter aim, we would have to say, was not the purpose of the biographical sketch and analysis.)

I will use as a base for this discussion some of the materials already presented on the case of Larry which appear in chapter 3. The reader is referred to the following passages given in chronological order: (1) October 2, 1968, p. 39; (2) September 25 to December 8, 1968, pp 45-52; (3) January 28, 1970, pp. 29-34; (4) April 15, 1970, pp. 36-37. If other data are referred to, they will be given in this section; otherwise the reader will be referred to the passages outlined above.

Larry's Conceptualizations about Making Art

(p. 39) Larry tries to invent "pen figures" which are equivalent to discriminations he perceives in nature. He wonders how to show light with black pen lines. He seems to conclude: "I can invent medium-tool devices tentatively equivalent to my visual impressions."

(p. 45) Concept: The artist can be master of the world out there which he is trying to represent. He can change sizes, tilt objects, leave items out, etc.

(p. 47) Concept: "Pen figures" can represent *simultaneously* more than one visual impression—e.g., "If I use wriggly lines which vary in weight and density I can represent *both* the texture of a tree trunk and the degree of light and shadow present at the same time."

(p. 48) Concept: Technical mastery, basic discipline, as in a craft, precedes satisfactory representation, which in turn is the basis for "expression." "If I can use the hammer and saw I can build something I want to."

(p. 48) Concept: Just as texture and light can be merged into one problem, so technical control and expressive qualities can be seen as interdependent, not separate, problems. "I can work at both feeling and technique together."

(p. 48) Concept: The right texture *and* form can be represented by direct pen strokes if one visualizes the whole first. Forms in nature need not be represented by a bounded outline. "I can organize a lot of complexity if I remain open and keep my eye on the whole I am after. Techniques within a given drawing must be consistent. I can't draw the lips with a tight outline if nothing else is."

(pp. 48-49) Concept: The projection of a solid like a head in a drawing requires spatial strategies. Related concept: A clear failure in representation can pinpoint a difficulty and bring it to consciousness. "I made the angle of the features different from the angle of the head as a whole, but the proper angle of the face is a reference point that should lead to a correction of that."

(p. 48) Spatial representation requires conceptual mastery, not just trying to copy what's out there.

(p. 51) Quick sketches and incomplete drawings can move one more fully toward solutions of representational problems. "I guess I loosened up a bit. I really was tight."

(p. 50) Concept: The world of art is much broader, much more exciting than the problems of representational mastery. "'Guernica' blew my mind. I saw too vastly different exhibitions (Flavin, Montenegro). The idea of art cannot be restricted. Yet all of these experiences were pleasant."

(p. 50) Concept: Confidence and feeling on the artist's part are an essential part of art expression. "That part which is mine alone, which I have strong feelings about, is important in art, just as it is in the art of others I enjoy."

(pp. 50-51) Concept: There are modes of drawing which are more abstract which communicate visually as well as or better than representational ones. "I have done something not so much concerned with realism—a visual experience, something different."

(pp. 50-51) Concept: Once one becomes liberated from realism only, interested in free exploration of media, in visual experiences which are different, in responding to the full range of art appreciatively, and in allowing a drawing to have levels of meaning which need not be pinned down, the world of expression and feeling opens up for him. "It is more of an effect, a visual experience, rather than just a representation."

(p. 29) Concept: Visual impressions and the feelings they arouse can be captured through explorations with media and tools in the act of expression. "I think I could get the lacey effect of trees against the gray sky with quick, thin brush strokes without applying too much pressure."

(p. 32) Concept: Reflection on the analogical, metaphorical quality of visual impressions aids one's efforts of expression. "I wanted to have them look like they are tumbling. It didn't look like a ramshackle house but as kind of opposed to a solid brick house . . . like an old wooden shack that was half crushed in . . . kind of bent out of shape."

(pp. 32-34) Concept: The mood pervading a place can be captured in a drawing of it (the Ebervale Post Office). Guided by feeling, one learns what to represent and how to do it. "I didn't bring the black coal dumps down to the roof. I just thought it looked better that way. It was kind of like a flatter type of thing. Kind of a flat behind a flat. Here it is not just a visual thing but kind of an image of a feeling."

(p. 33) Concept: Ideas will come without forcing them and will come while working. "It was the mood way. I was doodling and all of a sudden there was something there. Everything kind of went around it from there."

(February 4, 1970. This is new material not available from sections of chap. 3) Concept: Exploration of media, tools, and the textures and spaces on a page are interesting in and of themselves, without guidance of a mood or visual impression beforehand. "I used a swirling kind of stroke and played around with the brush. I tried to get interesting spaces in between as I went along, to catch the eye and give movement. It was not just exploring the form but the medium too."

(February 4, 1970. New material) Concept: Methods used earlier can be used again but on a higher level, with new ingredients which extend them. (On November 20, 1968, Larry did a drawing which was pure brush experimentation. He made a gridwork then used different brushes, different strokes, differing amounts of water and ink within them. On February 4, 1970, the exploration of medium was not tied to a rigid division of the page, but was part of an open exploration of space, movement, form, and texture.) "I just kept doing something, developing without anything special in mind. I was just sort of trying to feel out the brush and do things with it."

(February 11, 1970. New material). Concept: There are complex interactions between experiences, associations and drawing processes. Example: Larry drew a pistol without a hand or background, pointing directly at the observer of his drawing. On the way to the drawing lab he ran into an acquaintance who was going to teach in a black school and was going to carry a gun to school. He visualized the pistol as a heavy, massive, black, cold object, at point-blank range—a machine that almost activated itself without a human will attached to it. He picked up a chisel shaped brush and used only it, a square tip, to construct very carefully the black, rounded forms (see fig. 8).

"I didn't realize what I was getting myself into until I made that first stroke, then I knew. It was kind of like an extra discipline for me." (The process emerged but the image was a strong guiding one from the start.) "I had the visual image when I was talking with this kid, and it just kind of hit me. It was a terrifying thing. I just felt that this gun was pointing right at me." (Larry had used a pistol just once before.) "I didn't like it very much—I don't like what it does to me. I can't find any relationship between what I do with it and myself. It is almost like —that thing there, almost commands itself. It's a free agent. It is so easy to shoot something. I didn't really conceive that I could do it. I even shot a turtle one time with a rifle, and it was so mechanical I didn't feel like I did it. Like somebody else did."

(February 25, 1970. New material.) Concept: Reflection can build up the idea of how one's successful drawings are held together. (Larry begins to conceptualize the ways he likes to go about drawing or painting.) "I think I start out with some kind of idea in my mind but with only the bare idea about it. Sort of a structure. . . . Kind of an organization before I start out. I get the things that are set in my mind, and from there I kind of develop around it. I kind of rely a bit on the brush, you know, and how things are turning out. . . . The feeling is kind of the whole thing. Right from the start, from the structure to the different things I have in my mind visually that I want to try to work out, that feeling is always the kind of main drive. Kind of holds it together."

(February 25, 1970. New material.) Concept: A transaction occurs between drawing, the medium, and real-life experience. Example: Larry at many points mentions becoming more sensitively aware of his visual environment (e.g., the greenness of the grass and the shapes in it, or how black the doorway is in a saloon entrance.) He also responds to qualities of medium for their own sake (e.g., how he liked a stroke which went from dark and wet to lighter and dry, almost around an entire form; or how good it felt to lay on dabs of thick plastic gray paint).

(April 8, 1970. New material.) Concept: The artist can abstract out the qualities he feels exist in his most successful drawings. (Larry reviews his work from the

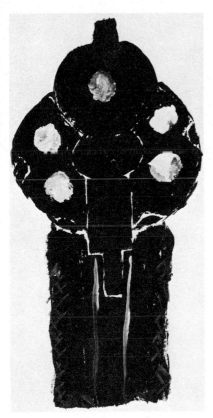

Figure 8.   Larry's drawing of gun

second 10-week series.) "They are stark. A lot of the others are spread all over the paper. . . . In these there is some kind of an impact." (He finds similar qualities in an exhibition he just saw.) "The ones I liked took a simple thing, like maybe galoshes near a sink, and maybe just the visual thing was captured. They were just there . . . I wouldn't say the lines so much but the shapes that were used to make it. It made a powerful image when you looked at it. It was something striking."

(April 8, 1970. New material.) Concept: The artist need not feel he is trapped in a single line of development. (Larry does not feel he must convince himself that he is always "developing.") "Each one is a different exploration. They don't culminate in anything."

(April 8, 1970. New material.) Concept: In-process development and interaction, or a dialogue with a drawing as it evolves, is an accepted way of working. Larry's explanation: "Even the stark ones were done in-process. The shapes came out differently than I planned to at first." (Question to Larry: "Even with the gun?") "The gun I let go its own way. I started with the position of the barrel, and even with that, I expanded the side of the barrel until I felt it was big enough or strong enough. I just built around it."

(April 8, 1970. New material.) Concept: It is possible to conceptualize about what is "purely visual" in art. Larry's explanation: "When I think of some of the great art, it gives you such a strong visual sense in one way or another. They were so aware of what they were seeing." Different example: "You might be driving along in a car or walking along, or just sitting, and happen to glance at something. . . . It just somehow, I don't know, falls together. Almost by accident." Further example: "I think it is a combination of mood and physical condition. . . . Not going around in a half-ass way, at a lower level of awareness, not being fully alive, not being all that perceptive. I used to think of it as kind of an animal-like awareness. It is just a superhuman awareness. You are just kind of really alive in a human way; you are seeing things and not just letting things go by. . . . The gun hit me that way."

(April 8, 1970. New material.) Concept: One can perceive himself as an artist—not a "professional" but an artist nevertheless. Larry's reasoning: "I'm an artist. . . . Maybe not, quote, like Picasso—but I think everyone can be an artist, in their own way. . . . In the kind of expression they can work on. I think that raises a question. . . . That everyone *should* have the kind of experience, you know, of trying to . . . of expression. A kind of a good thing . . . for a human to do. . . . It affects the total life this way. You know [laughs], I look at these . . . I don't know if I'd hang them up in my apartment or not. Among you I could feel open, but maybe someone would look at them and 'Ycchh'. . . . You know its *nothing* but to *me* I can say it's bad but still there is something."

(pp. 36-37) Concept: Directed by a pervasive mood, an open attitude, and a dialectic of exploration of tools and media, new methods are invented by the artist during the on-going drawing process. In the example given on pp. 36-37, some technical innovations for Larry occur: The use of three different brushes for three different shades of black, white, and gray; the use of white on white to keep an open area solid, not empty; the use of suggestion, vagueness, undefined strokes in areas where emphasis should not detract from more important areas; making black something precious so it counts as something symbolic.

(April 15, 1970. New material.) Concept: The act of drawing is its own intense reality. Larry's example: "When you're in there, you are face to face with the visual problem. You can't just have some vague undefined thoughts. You've got to get right to it. You can't evade . . . I don't know what you are doing when you are drawing—your feelings, your perceptions, you have to be more aware of them."

Analysis

Already under that part of chapter 3 headed "Literary Psychology" (p. 43), I have attempted some interpretations, in the form of summaries of Larry's case. The reader is referred to the last two paragraphs of that example (pp. 51-52). At this point I am going to try to summarize with more brevity the twenty-six items representing Larry's conceptualizations of how he makes art. These are given in the order of their previous presentation.

1. The artist is the source of invention, selection, and mastery.

2. Drawing elements cognized separately interact, producing higher-order principles.

3. Skill is the basis upon which to build expression.

4. Skills and expression are interdependent.

5. Visualization of the whole can lead to sensitive handling of complex ideas and usher in a principle of consistency.

6. Specific failures reflected upon can pinpoint solutions.

7. Conceptualization guides representational efforts.

8. Relaxing control, quick sketches, and the like, can help solve some representational problems.

9. Art is pluralistic; many different qualities can be enjoyed.

10. The artist's confidence in himself and his own feelings guides his expression.

11. Departure from realism can in itself be expressive.

12. Visual phenomena have implicit meanings which, teased out as metaphors, guide expression.

13. A pervasive mood organizes and guides the drawing process.

14. Ideas must not be forced; with patience they come, in-process.

15. Medium and process without regard to representation and mood are intrinsically exciting.

16. Older drawing ideas can be redone on a higher level, as on a spiral.

17. Strong life experiences and the experience of the drawing process balance towards equivalence of structure.

18. Under a sufficient history of experience an artist can conceptualize his own consistent successful strategy and use it like a flexible plan.

19. Drawing experience and perception of the world interact to enhance each other.

20. Qualities of one's drawings perceived as successful can be abstracted and reflected upon as a kind of self-revelation.

21. While influenced by past drawings, one is free *not* to develop along a line; he can explore.

22. The dialogic, transformational nature of the art process is accepted and preferred.

23. Art has to do with things "purely visual" and with a heightened, special kind of perception.

24. One can see himself as an artist (though not a professional). This perception of a special artistic self is good for everyone.

25. Under a pervasive mood and open mind, new methods *will* emerge in-process.

26. The act of drawing is its own intense experiential encounter.

How shall I proceed to further analyze and interpret these conceptualizations, abstracted from a mass of material which spans more than two years? Let's play with some ground rules.

First, though, I want to acknowledge again that the twenty-six concepts just presented owe their origin to the basic questions I asked on pages 58-59. They are a function of my intuition as to what can, in an abstract way, describe dynamics of change in a series of drawings of a given individual where a special participant observer gains indirect access to the artist's stream of consciousness. Other quetions asked, by myself or by my research assistant (also a special participant observer), would eventuate in a different set of abstracted concepts.

So, the first influence, which is one not showing and one therefore not easily criticized, is that established by the basic set taken toward the data, the history, as a whole. Second, guided by that set, the working conceptualizations which Larry holds at various times in the series are abstracted: at this point with more supporting evidence, in the form of things he said or implied. Third, these are rephrased in a brief, direct statement.

Now, how to proceed? The time-line can be examined to see how the concepts distribute themselves in time (the points are in chronological order). Against this time-line, that is, further or more abstract concepts can be played. Some of these are fairly obvious.

Illustration: How conscious is Larry of his own drawing series or drawing history, and how does this consciousness enter into his conceptualizations about making art? I feel that six of the points (16, 18, 19, 20, 21, 24) clearly refer to conceptualizations dependent on the cumulative nature of the series. Some of these are fairly obvious (16, 18, 20); others are subtle (19, 21, 24). They all occur, as would be expected, toward the latter part of the time-line.

But these same points can be absorbed into other questions equally well (still with reference to the time-line). Suppose we raise the more abstract question of Larry's emerging consciousness of an artistic self-identity. Here my eye would pick out a larger number of points, and these would incorporate the six already listed under "series effect" (8, 10, 14, 15, *16*, 17, *18, 19, 20, 21*, 22, *24*, 26; the series effect points are *italicized*). Again, these occur "with time." They show attitudes and in-process thinking which conceives of making art as a dynamic, interactive dialogue between image, feeling, and medium.

In fact, if I look at the points for what I would call "in-process thinking" (indicated by 10, 13, 14, 15, 18, 22, 25, 26) and combine these with the earlier "drawing series effect" (16, 18, 19, 20, 21, 24), I would pretty well account for Larry's emerging artistic self-identity, as I have picked it out (only three points out of fifteen would fail to merge into "artistic self-identity" when "series" and "process" are combined). I am not making a strong case for this play with numbered points, for it is not a statistical procedure at all but a way of speaking more abstractly about a greater number of concepts than the mind can manipulate simultaneously. I cannot keep fifteen points in mind at one time, but I can indicate that what I feel represents Larry's emerging "artistic self-identity" is composed largely of the stable cumulative history of his own drawings (which he is able to reflect on, interconnect, and evaluate over a recorded series so that he can conceptualize that very series as regards qualities of drawings, strategies of drawing, his freedom or determined nature in the series, and the like) and of his consciousness of "in-process thinking" and his acceptance thereof. It seems all too bald, but I am saying that for Larry it looks as though his artistic self-identity is comprised of consciousness of a history of making art and a movement toward in-process thinking.

Still other concepts occur toward the latter part of the time-line. Larry speaks of art-life interactions (17, 19, 23). He becomes conscious of the guiding power of feeling and mood (10, 13, 17, 19, 23, 25). He plays with what might be called a nascent "theory of art" (9, 11, 12, 15, 17, 20, 23, 24, 26). And he responds to what I have called "idiosyncratic meaning" (4, 10, 11, 12, 13, 14, 16, 17, 20). He also gives evidence of a capacity for "inner drawing" (4, 5, 7, 16, 18, 20, 21). Many of these points overlap with the large "artistic self-identity" category. Certainly if one can cognize his own drawing history, is developing an open theory of art, is aware of idiosyncratic meaning, mood and feeling, sees art and life as transactionally interdependent, and tends toward in-process dynamics, then he is constructing a viable artistic self-identity, I would ague. In so saying, I realize I put value connotations on top of what was at first an effort merely to play categories against Larry's conceptualizations about making art, as these were arranged on a time-line.

But Larry had some things "going for him" from the start. If I pick out points concerning "artistic causality" (1, 5, 7, 8, 10, 11, 16, 18, 20, 21, 22, 24), or "intentional symbolization" (1, 7, 10, 12, 13, 16, 17, 20, 23), or indicators of "confidence over fear" (1, 4, 5, 6, 7, 8, 10, 11, 12, 13, 14, 15, 16, 19, 20, 21, 22, 24, 25, 26), then, as the reader can see, these spread throughout the twenty-six points rather evenly. This would indicate that Larry entered into the thirty weeks of self-instructed drawing (spread over two and one-half years) with an attitude that could be adjudged favorable to change toward an emerging artistic self-identity, open to dynamic, interactive forces within the art process itself. He saw himself as an active force, capable of taking liberties with the medium and with the world "out there." He had feelings, ideas, and purposes consciously in mind from the start which he wished to express, and these were not wildly out of line with what he might hope to do. While not always happy with his efforts, he did not seem afraid to try new things. He felt relatively secure and confident. One is reminded of some of the research in psychotherapy which suggests that those showing marked improvement often have, from the start, a greater degree of self-insight and empathy, and a more favorable self-attitude, than those not showing comparable improvement. It is as though a weak signal is picked up and amplified.

What, however, is the specific history of Larry's changes in his conceptualizations about art and making art? Quite early (point 2) he found that "elements" (such as different "pen-figures") invented separately interacted to form new super-elements or methods (light-shade and texture were not independent representational problems). In like manner, he had to revise his first notion that skill preceded expression (point 3) and acknowledge that skill and expression were part of the "dialectics" of drawing, influencing each other (point 4). He learned to envision and plan the whole drawing to a degree, which, coupled with an eye on how the parts come together, allowed him to handle complex ideas in a consistent manner (point 5). At this time he was limited to representational drawing. He realized, however, that mastery of such drawing skills was not a matter of capturing the illusion of appearances, but required his abiltiy to conceive of space and solids, for example (point 7), to try an idea out and learn later what went wrong (point 6), and to explore in more relaxed manner alternative representations (point 8).

Nevertheless, as our data from the interviews with Larry show, he was feeling depressed and tight even while slowly mastering representational skills and his power to visualize, explore, and conceptualize in this drawing mode. He then learns, very quickly to an observer's eye, three important concepts: art has many faces and these are to be responded to and enjoyed each in its own way (point 9); the artist centers his faith on his inner feelings rather than on skills for representing what's "out there" (point 10); and, furthermore, the very departure from what's "out there" is in itself loaded with expressive potential (point 11). The account (pp. 50-52) indicates some of the specific life-art events concurrent with these rather dramatic changes. (From my view, Larry's history up to this point would not have "predicted" such a noticeable shift or transformation.)

Thereafter, some consolidation of this changed view toward art takes place. These are less dramatic, but important for self-direction. He plays with the analogical, metaphorical aspect of visual phenomena (point 12), and allows symbolic aspects of drawings to float freely, not pinned down. Not just visualization but feeling and mood guide and integrate complex drawings (point 13), and even interact with the power to imagine. He handles himself like a responsive, trusted instrument which must not be forced but which will respond in action (point 14). He is willing to set aside representation and even mood (as associations with objects and places experienced) to explore those aspects of medium, tool, and evolving formal properties which are intrinsically interesting (point 15).

He sees that his own drawing history can be conceptualized (points 16, 18, 20) in a way which allows him to maximize his potential for expression, continuity, and mastery. Yet he need not be determined by his past. Drawings can explore new alternatives because one is conscious of older solutions; they need not culminate deterministically in the next logical development (point 21). He finds art both more fun and exciting, but also more serious and demanding. Art and life interact (points 17, 19) more and more, and Larry develops a conceptualization about things "purely visual" which guides him in his drawings and influences him toward a heightened perception of the world around him.

Finally, he accepts the open, changing dialogue which is creation in art (point 22), trusting that he and his methods will evolve and be transformed in process (point 25). The act of drawing becomes an encounter, a reality all of its own (point 26) and Larry knows that he is (and when he is) an artist, though without professional pretensions. He thinks that this is intrinsically valuable and good, not only for himself but probably for everyone.

(Parenthetically, at this point in his life, Larry graduated from college and was drafted into the army and sent to Vietnam. He returned to the drawing laboratory once just before going overseas. It was at a time when we had just put out another student's work for a review of a ten-week period of drawings. Larry knew that he could not respond sensitively to what was on the wall without much more knowledge of the student's thinking, intentions, and feelings—without sharing that specific drawing series as a special history. Larry also wondered whether there was a place in art education for people like him, for he felt he had become sensitive to the whole problem of nurturing art expression in others through doing so in himself. This is where our knowledge of Larry ends, at least for this point in time.)

We have seen, in review, the development of a strengthened sense of artistic self-identity in Larry, nurtured in the matrix of his own cumulative drawing actions and in the review of these by interested but counter-intervening special participant observers. Apart from the peculiar conditions obtaining in the drawing laboratory, it appears that Larry's artistic self-identity overlaps with his consciousness of his own series history and with his gradual acceptance of in-process thinking within the drawing act itself. Undergirding the above "difficult" and highly abstract conceptualizations about his making art, we find Larry aware of changes in his perception occasioned by his immersion in art; we see that his own experiences and feelings guide him through a drawing; and we see that he can draw "inside his head" as time goes on, and tease out meanings peculiarly his own. He also enlarges his concept of art to include much more than representation. Larry began with a "good attitude" toward himself and art, but nevertheless had to come to a kind of crisis where he transcended his self-imposed limitations (even though he had been developing within his own rules). He moves beyond representation toward symbolized feeling, toward the "purely visual," and to the dynamic aspects of medium and the forming process. He utilizes himself as an instrument responsive within an encounter. He knows that he is an artist. He knows when he is an artist.

Summary of the Historical Modes

I have spent some time presenting a partial case history as illustrative of an effort at historical analysis and interpretation. I have tried to revive the events of that history on an abstract level. I have tried to escape from a historical determinism which projects the idea of an antecedent-consequence kind of causality. What has emerged is admittedly a function of Larry's stream of consciousness as reconstructed through stimulated recall and of my experience as a special participant observer who shared that history by direct observation and by interaction within the recall inquiry sessions. I was present at the birth of the conceptualizations presented. While I feel they are Larry's, I acknowledge my role, and the role of the drawing laboratory procedures, in bringing them to consciousness. I also acknowledge that the wording of the concepts as they finally appear in this analysis is mine, as is the analysis and interpretation of them.

The ultimate objective of such a presentation is that of understanding and appreciating a history of change of a given artistic serial. While conditioned, contingent, and determined from one point of view, from the point of view of the artist's consciousness the artistic serial is open, proactive, superstatic. Artistic causality, intentional symbolization, idiosyncratic meaning, and a growing artistic self-identity are assumed to be realities of that serial, existentially considered. The artistic and the creative emerge within this history of a live creature in a particular kind of world.

Procedurally, I have operated much as does a critic or historian, who describes, analyzes, and interprets. The process is as follows: assumption ⟶ designation and description ⟶ appropriate data ⟶ establishment of explicit set or of ground rules for interpretation ⟶ abstraction according to guiding set or ground rules, with evidence supporting the abstracted properties ⟶ simplification of abstracted properties into still more abstract form (for ease of manipulation) ⟶ analysis by comparisons, sequences, reflections against a time-line, development of superordinate concepts, and the like (all of this guided by the set or the ground rules) ⟶ summarization and interpretation ⟶ critique of the process.

Please note again, in closing this section, that, according to the basic assumptions of this book, it is a special kind of history with which we are concerned. What may well seem like naïve historical method on my part must be read against the acceptance of the existential and phenomenological validity of inquiry based upon indirect access to the active artist's stream of consciousness through a special participant observer, and focused upon a series of works produced in a known environment. The reader may not accept the "primitive terms" upon which this work is erected. Nevertheless, critiques of the alternatives presented herein must accept these assumptions as a starting point, or they will not help, as I hope they will, the clarification of methods so based. It is neither a strict positivism nor a pervasive subjectivism (rationalism, idealism) that guides this effort, but rather, as Van Kaam effectively indicates, the acceptance of man as both contingent and free, as concerned with meaning and value in his experience in the world.[18] We are creatures who deal symbolically with our own experiencing. The existence of art as a dynamic process guided by an agent finding his path in the expressive act in the real world is the ground concept we must accept. Else there is no art and we study something else. The artist is not a rock, but a man creating meaning.

Existential-phenomenological Reconstruction and Analysis of the Drawing Process

In this mode a closer look is taken of the reconstructed drawing process utilizing the artist's stimulated recall of the drawing plus the special participant observer's enlargement of the subjective frame of reference through an effort to show linkages between the psychic events within the artist and observable external events. The latter are to be read as process feedback (and its likely transformation within the artist), interruptions, special medium changes and difficulties, suggestions from others, spread-effect from previous drawings, and the like.

As in the historical mode just presented, the set or viewpoint of the researcher is quite important to the presentation and analysis and should be made as explicit as possible. The general method is akin to the multiple-consciousness narrative of chapter 3, except that now the effort is less narrative and more contingent on the artist's and the special participant observer's roles and the privileged viewpoints and inferences proper to each. In general, as I approach this task, I am still operating largely as counsel in the artist's defense, but I bring to bear other concepts which I cannot disown without giving up my very perception of the external events and of the psychic events which are to be reconstructed and analyzed.

The set toward which I am inclined might be called one stressing "artistic-expressive cybernetics." By this I mean that I am inclined to focus upon the transactional process whereby the artist's intention (idea, feeling, or imagery, with its attendant implicit, idiosyncratic meaning) is projected by some selective initial strategy or act, recycled and evaluated as in-process feedback, transformed in both symbolic and procedural ways, and on into a new cycle or transformation selection or application, action, feedback, and so on. I choose this model because I believe that it best fits the drawing process. Whereas in my earlier work, I studied drawing strategies and conditions affecting them, and therefore took a more objective, external reference point, I now seek to play the subjective-objective conditions, as reconstructed, against each other; for drawing is neither one nor the other. While overwhelmingly subjective and covert from one point of view, it nevertheless occurs in the real world where drawings get begun, developed, torn up, or finished; where the hand pushes or draws or strokes a soft carbon pencil, for example, on *this* sheet of paper, in *this* kind of setting, and where the drawing in question was preceded and followed by another, as part of one person's artistic serial.

When, therefore, I attempt an existential-phenomenological reconstruction and analysis of the drawing process, I am no longer the special participant observer, but an inquirer at still a higher level of abstraction who reflects on all of the material—the mute evidence (especially the drawings adjacent in a series, and the in-process time-lapse photos of the drawing selected for analysis), the inquiry attempting to share the artist's stream of consciousness as recalled under the stimulus of his own reviewed processes, and the observers' "laboratory notes" which indicate perceived structure in the recall and contingencies within the environment.

It is true that phenomenological observers often state that they try to set aside "assumptions" while they put all their energy into "attending" to their "feelings" vis-à-vis the phenomena of concern. Still, as I have earlier indicated, the very process of symbolization of the "attended-to-feelings" is one which, while not arbitrary, is selective, representative, and partial, and this is of necessity. I chose terms such as "image," "intention," "feedback," "transformation," and the like, because these seem representative of my *more abstract reflections* on my own drawing processes and those of others whose processes I can to some privileged degree share. Therefore, even while attempting to attend to the unique drawing process upon which I focus, I attend to its uniqueness as fitting and departing from some mind set (which for the reader and for the sake of analysis I feel should be made explicit). An ambiguity creeps in here because I cannot attend without some set, even as my perceptual apparatus itself so operates. Yet in transaction with the phenomena, through reflection on my feelings, I can clarify and revise that set. Further, even my "raw data," especially my "laboratory notes" and my questions to the artist during the inquiry on process recall, have within them implicit but less conscious views, on my part. While these can be themselves the subject of an analysis, I am inclined to accept them as "the given" upon which further analysis will be performed. I operated thus in the historical mode given earlier in this chapter.

In order to save space, I am again going to use material presented earlier in this book as the basis for a beginning effort in this mode. The reader is referred to the "first-person-singular narrative" example (pp. 36-37) in which Larry's depiction of a downtown section of Baltimore is described (fig. 4 reproduces this drawing). As a further basis for new reflections on this drawing, eighteen time-lapse process shots of the evolution of Larry's drawing are presented in figure 9. I will also draw upon a transcription of the inquiry session which immediately followed the drawing, stimulated by the replay of the videotape which recorded the entire drawing's history. (This transcription was the basis for the "first-person-singular narrative" on pp. 36-37.) The sequences of the drawing will be referred to according to the eighteen process samples given in figure 9 (as "photo 1," etc.).

(Photos 1, 2, 3, 4, 5) In this sequence Larry lays in the central subject of the scene, the building with the bar on the street level. He begins with broad quick strokes of a flat brush, allowing the paint to change from loaded to dry brush. Already in photo 2 he has set down the crudely lettered "Bar" sign and the frame of the door beneath it. By photo 4 the partly opened door and the blackness inside the bar are suggested and the tones spread to the undescribed building beyond the bar entrance. Larry wanted to convey the feeling he was right in the midst of this street scene, and that it was overpowering. I thought he was viewing it at first from up above, but he corrected me. He said: "The feeling I had was not being above, by any means. It was being . . . everything was stronger than me, sort of."

His first strokes (photos 1, 2) were meant to get down in open fashion, the main idea. "I was trying to use stronger, bolder strokes," he said in the inquiry session, adding with an implied negative evaluation, "but you just need a lot more practice to do it." He admitted that the first strokes were a base to work within—kind of a foothold. These strokes retain their beginning identity until photo 10 when they begin to expand into a probe to determine what those buildings are like above the street level, over the bar, and the "Naked Show" which gets sketched in by photo 6 and labeled finally by photo 9 (impressionistic sign). The billboards do not get a suggestion of a burlesque-type figure until photo 17. The bar, by photo 4, is described: "It has an open entrance with the darkness around it."

"This is open here, you mean?" I asked.

"Yeah, and you see the darkness," Larry replied. "Terrifying! These bars are darker than any I've ever seen. It confounded me, sort of. I put real heavy white strokes on it . . . thick."

The white strokes refer to the sidewalk which gets laid in by photo 6, just as the decorative marquee of the burlesque house was outlined. What drew Larry to the sidewalk at this point? Was it to establish a feeling for "ground" or was it the contrast of outside and sidewalk with the darkness inside the bar. Perhaps it was the next extension to work within later, much as the only partially committed strokes of "building above the bar" had been.

Larry helped answer some of my questions: "Well, I was kind of looking for contrast. I didn't want a white sidewalk in Baltimore, by any means; I did dirty them up a bit. I wanted to get that . . . it was feeling good—the paint was feeling good right there."

By photo 8 the dark entrances to the burlesque house and two framing billboards are painted in, and at 9, as indicated, "Naked Show" appears on the marquee. During this sequence, Larry pauses to consider what to do next. He says that a lot of things were going on in his mind.

"When you say 'a lot of things'—were you thinking ahead as well as of what you were doing?" I asked.

Figure 9. Process shots of Larry's Baltimore scene

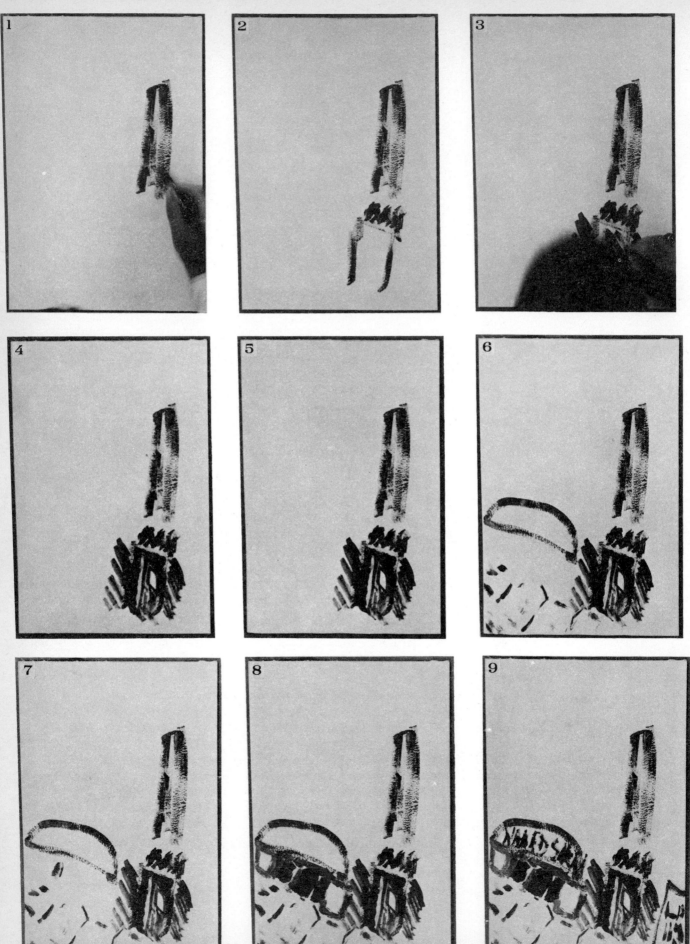

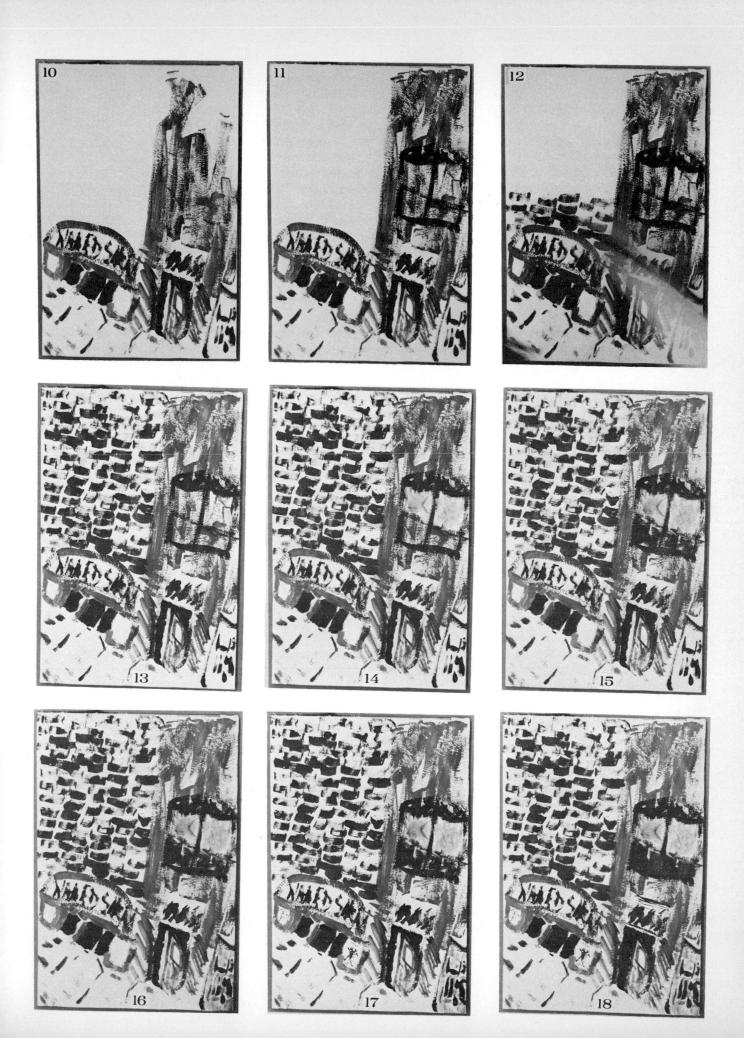

Larry replied: "I was kind of getting hit with all kind of possibilities of improving my technique, of expanding the things that I'm doing. I could see . . . later on, not here so much, a little later I was struck with the idea of getting a different color. These colors, these shades, are limited here. First of all, I thought I'd like to use some red, or some brown. I was working on something there, and I thought 'maybe if I give it a little touch of white.' "

"Like you're tinting a color?" I asked.

"Yeah, like if I drew this here, just to highlight it with a little bit of white . . . not so it's noticeable, but it just kind of works on the eye in an unconscious way."

Larry, then, refers to direct strokes, to improving his technique, to the plastic quality of heavy white strokes, and to the feeling of "color" and how he could represent it with his black and white acrylic paints. At the same time as these procedural concerns were on his mind, they were process developments and not the end of his efforts, for he was guided by a strong feeling of the presence of that environment with him in the middle of it. As in prior drawings, when he tries to suggest "feeling" or "mood" he seems to evoke a criterion of what is consistent throughout, but he also tries to suggest feeling by the very way he handles the medium. He tells me during the inquiry: "If you look at it carelessly, you can see it a lot better."

It seems, thus, that Larry wants to keep his painted drawing somewhat vague, suggestive, or impressionistic. I could not read the signs above the bar and burlesque at first, for example. He also wants to pull things out of the vagueness only when they become symbolic or can really count—things like the blackness of the entrances or the solidity of the sidewalks.

He did not really want to be impressionistic he told me, but literal—literal in the way that caught his feelings: "It's like—like, when I see things that kind of strike me, it's not an impressionistic blur—it's cold—it's not cold, that implies an emotional feeling—but it's there, you know, it's for real."

"A stark kind of feeling?" I asked, because he had referred to such a purely "visual" quality before.

"Yeah, I wanted to get that, because I think it's true to the way I feel about it. At the same time I wanted to get these strokes, you know?"

"This modulation between the strokes and this feeling, this visual effect, you're trying to get?"

"You see, by the strokes I was trying to get some of the forms, the shapes and . . . I think I'm seeing a little more strongly than when I first started painting—a little more, like aware. I can't even explain it. Sometimes it hits me like, I see things like—let's see—like walking up—I'll give you an example—walking up here this morning, I was so aware that the grass is green. It's like, in front of the Hub, there were shapes in the grass. Like the trees, you know, the limbs, the heavier limbs, there were some maples."

Larry then corroborated that handling the drawing medium and tools interacted with this developing visual sense. "Yeah, I think they're related . . . like this is somehow developing my awareness."

"The acts of perception and the acts of painting kind of mix together?"

"Yeah. You see these forms and things I saw walking up here in State College, and the atmosphere, the clean air, nature, and safe feeling."

So this was in Larry's mind that morning, as a contrast with Baltimore. "It really hit me," he said of that contrast. "The forms were all too much for a man to handle. The only people that could exist were broken-down whores and bums that drank . . . what were they drinking? Adrura port, or something like that. These are broken-down people, you know. That's the only people you see . . . you just don't live there without getting affected."

I dwell on this description and on the contrast of that morning because these were apparently occasions of strong feeling and perception in Larry's experiencing, and he was struggling to make the drawing session symbolize some of this. Much is condensed, as in a dream, which is relevant to any given drawing.

By photo 9, changes occurred in the drawing I couldn't quite follow, so I asked: "This you brought in here, beside the bar door?"

"It says 'naked show.' I didn't care to make it real clear."

"I read it as kind of a theater entrance," I said.

"And a black door," Larry added, "It really didn't have a black door—but it kind of hit me that everything you looked into was black."

"The bar and the theater . . . and you're suggesting kind of the feelings of the people, too," I stated, trying to probe further for his meaning.

"Yeah," Larry reflected, "they're surrounded in this darkness."

By photo 10, Larry has completed, for the time being, the bar, the burlesque theater, and the sidewalk. He now returns to "that which is above the street floor." This had been left purposefully vague and undefined, although it was represented by the very first strokes laid down in photo 1. Now, in photo 10, he expands those initial strokes, widening them and containing them with a vertical area from the division between the bar and the burlesque to the top of the page. In photo 10 there is still no indication of the dormer-type window which appears by photo 11, but Larry allows the uncovered and scrubbed areas of the building façade to remain for incorporation into the window superimposed over it.

Larry described this sequence: "Here, I was getting down those grays [photos 10, 11], but they just didn't go along with the rest of the picture. I had to break it up a bit."

"You just didn't want to fill it in?" I asked, sensing a consistency principle being applied, gathered from the staccato and broken effect of the drawing up to now. "This is just like building above the bar?"

"Yeah. Like first floor, second floor—I don't know what they have up above, but it—everything from the ground up, is dingy."

"You didn't want it too defined?"

"No. You're kind of surrounded by these feelings, these walls."

"The kind of things you remember are like the blackness and the general dinginess?" I inquired.

"Yeah, and it's like that's the whole thing. Like even if you look up in the sky there's smog. In fact, you don't even have to look up, it's there. It's *on* you."

"There, said Larry, referring to the T.V. screen and the phase corresponding to photo 11, "I put a window in, kind of. I really didn't have anything in mind."

"A kind of dormer-like thing?"

"Yeah, a big old window. There's all kinds. You can really get into windows like that. Big windows like that on second floors are kind of interesting. They're all over the place and they're all different. I thought maybe it would, like, tie things together a little bit more."

Larry didn't like the plain gray, so he sorted through his mind and came up with the big window. He said he knew he had a lot of eye-catching stuff on the bottom and that he'd have to get "something to balance out the top and make it come together somehow."

By photo 12, Larry is trying to solve the problem of the untouched space above the burlesque theater in the upper left half of the page. He puts a few stroke marks down and studies it. "I looked at it, and it did something. I don't know what exactly." He settles on what he called "dash marks" (interestingly, he had used "dash marks" in with his "pen figures" two years before).

"I'm putting these dash marks—it's somehow appropriate, but I really don't know just what it elicits in me when I look at it. [These dash marks are laid in during photos 12, 13.] I started to think about it then and realized it was kind of an impressionistic type of thing, but it did something—I don't know what. Like, you know, the tops of these buildings are all different and I thought maybe I'd try to portray that this is, maybe, a large brownstone—something like that. I didn't really know but I thought I'd get maybe like a different shape in there."

Thus a change from a freely brushed, gray fill-in, over which a larger dormer is superimposed to "dash marks" symbolized different treatments for different kinds of buildings. He points out to me that he's working with bigger brushes and stronger strokes. He said, "I used a lot of power with the brush."

No discernible change occurs at first in photo 14. Larry is here contemplating his work. There is one change, however. The window shades on the large dormer window are made solid with whitish paint, to block out the tones of the building which were set down before the window was superimposed.

While watching the video tape playback I said to Larry: "I noticed that you brought in some white with the right hand and some dark with the left and did some on-the-sheet mixing here."

"Yeah, I had that white window shade and I wanted to get at—a tinge of gray."

I continued: "You hit it with the left hand with a few strokes of black, then you just kind of mixed them in. That's a new approach, in a sense, and your palette and approach permitted that."

"Like when I started out," Larry recalled, "I had that bigger palette. I didn't have any paint marks on it. How am I going to use this? I tried something different. I put a little pile of white here, of black here, like I've done since I started; but then I put a pile of gray in the middle. And I used three brushes. Before I was working almost exclusively with one brush and I had to work it out. . . . Like, I had the paper [scrap] over here, so I could keep the consistency the way I wanted it—not too runny or heavy. Like I made one movement—it was this door here—I put in a black sopping wet. I wiped it off because it didn't do what I wanted it to."

"That's where you got the towel," I observed. "You like your paint usually with some body to it?"

"Yeah. I'm just touching up there a bit," said Larry pointing to the video tape replay. "I want to keep consistent what I've been doing with this picture, yet I somehow wanted to touch it off a little bit—it didn't look quite done," still referring to the video tape. "But I didn't want to introduce some new things, you know, and break up the consistency. Like, I could have gotten a little bit too literal, or I could have used different shades that would have broken it up."

As we get to photos 13-18, then, the overt action slows down, as Larry reflects on how to unify and finish his picture in a consistent way.

"At the time of photo 17 I observed: "You put some touches on these little billboards too."

"Yeah, I put some white on there, then some gray." said Larry, repeating a process he had used on the window shades. "Plain paper [laughs]—I'm pretty conscious of the plastic quality of the paint. It disturbs me if . . . I'd rather have white [paint] there than white paper." There, Larry referred again to the video tape, "I'm just touching up a bit. Like, geeze, it looks too impressionistic. Not really definite things, because I thought if I got too definite it would have broken it up."

"You still use what I'll call . . . 'suggestion lines.' You don't want to be able to go up to it with a magnifying glass and say, 'oh, it's that.' "

"Get something just by looking at it—at the whole thing," said Larry.

"You've done that with the signs over the doors, too, haven't you?"

"Yeah." Larry paused as he watched the video tape playback, "those empty spaces bother me."

I recalled that at this point I had interrupted him so that we would have time for an instant replay of his drawing before another artist came into the lab.

"Well," he reflected, "when you came in I was just about to tackle the window. You didn't hurt it—I was at a loss anyway."

"Did you do more to the window?"

"I think I put a little more black in it—underneath the shades. Kind of . . . to be consistent with the idea of blackness inside."

Actually, the darkness beneath the window shades came in by photo 15, before the billboards at the burlesque theater were tackled (photo 17).

I referred to the end stages (photos 16-18): "I see you're working on those white spaces where they just kind of stand out—just white paper. That's interesting. Your strokes remain but the white paper recedes out of there."

"I guess I tried to get some sort of . . . it's kind of hard to do when you're using only three basic colors, to use one of your colors as a kind of controlling type thing —like the blackness inside the building compared to the 'grungieness' outside," mused Larry. (By "colors" he means "values.") He continued: "Maybe if I had more colors I could have concentrated more on using the blacks here and here and here . . . but. . . ." He pointed to the black doors and the black under the window shades.

"To make them stand out even more than they do?"

"Yeah. But it doesn't work that well in this situation. Black, white, and grays."

At this point our time was up, for another artist was entering the lab for a working session.

Contextualism and Structuralism as Supportive of Presented Alternative Modes

So terminates this exercise in reconstruction of the drawing process from what I have called an existential-phenomenological perspective. Actually, I suppose I am continually operating from what Pepper calls a contextualist world view.[19] This can be seen from the fact that I am resistant to *a prioristic* stances, even though I own up to the fact that all descriptions entail perspectives. My feeling that art must be grasped from the artist's side if we are to comprehend its formation has made me insistent upon the basic primitive terms of my approach (shared access to the artist's reconstructed stream of consciousness under a special participant observer's role). Even my effort at a historical mode was more reconstruction than interpretation, although I did at least clarify the set under which I engaged in abstractive processes.

The historic event, as Pepper says, is the root metaphor of contextualism; and the theory to which it commits one is synthetic and not analytical. By "historic event," Pepper explains,

> the contextualist does not mean primarily a past event, one that is, so to speak, dead and has to be exhumed. He means the event alive in its present. . . . The real historic event, the event in its actuality, is when it is going on *now*, the dynamic dramatic active event. We may call it an "act," if we like, and if we take care of our use of the term. But it is not an act conceived as alone or cut off that we mean; it is an act in and with its setting, an act in its context.[20]

Pepper goes on to say that we should use only verbs in talking of the contextualist view of the world: doing, making, creating, laughing, and the like. Such acts or events are extremely complex, with patterns that are continuously changing.[21]

Further, disorder is "a categorical feature of contextualism, and so radically so that it must not even exclude order." And in focusing on the "total given event" in all its concreteness, richness and complexity, an uncommon degree of arbitrariness exists in why one feature is selected rather than another.[22] (Hence what I called the "Roshomon effect" in chap. 2.) Concreteness (or what in chap. 2 I referred to as "concrete particularizing givens"), uniqueness and wholeness have been set out as singularly appropriate concepts upon which to concentrate in the description of expressive acts. Perhaps academic psychology has made too much of "permanent structures" in nature and in behavior, on the one hand, whereas art has made too much of change and novelty, on the other. I have veered more toward the latter, in keeping with my contextualist stance closer to the phenomena my special view allows me to reconstruct and, it is to be hoped, revitalize, as regards the expressive act itself.

The structure of a given expressive act, then, is seen as peculiar, though inexhaustible, in its very concreteness. I have lately been fond of saying that we can never know the expressive act, but that we can indeed study it, if only indirectly, and through a concern with its context and structure we can do two things: arrive at an understanding and appreciation of it, and reflect upon it from some more abstract and theoretical vantage point. These two aims, though interrelated, are distinct and different. They drive us toward considerations of context and of structure. At this point in my own intellectual life, I am closer to the context side, but I acknowledge considerations of structure. The very fact that I study not just one expresive act but a series by a given artist inclines me to a view wherein the "form" of the series incorporates the individual processes or expressive acts as their "content." The series still remains a lived history contextually explored, but it raises, at least synthetically, the kinds of "speculations" I refer to in the next section dealing with "the particular theorizing mode: the type concept." It does not, however, plunge me willy-nilly into the transcendental world of essences, as Husserlian phenomenology would have it. I skirt "thin atomism" in the reductive, behavioristic, mechanistic, positivistic methods (to which the modes herein are an alternative), on the one side, and a "fat gestaltism," or an excessively narrow phenomenology, Platonist in flavor, on the other.

Therefore, as I play at modes I only budge so far: they are deflections from a basically empirical and contextualist base predicated on the two massive procedural assumptions of this work.

To return to our contextualist view, it may be said that the structures of concern have been those alive in the series or the process under view. Continuity *outside* the context has not been assumed, except in the weakest and most inescapable manner. I have only permitted myself to speculate (next section) as to whether the structure of Larry's series encourages us to entertain a theory about how untrained college undergraduate artists guide themselves in making their art. Certainly any "case" I have studied impresses me with its uniqueness and its lawfulness simultaneously. Whether the particular lawfulness resonates with that of another series is a matter for exploration and for elucidation as to what level of abstraction and what method is involved.

Whatever the reader thinks of my arbitrary focus on a given expressive act, he can hardly deny that I deal with its real structure as a historic event. The concern is with behavior: observed, shared, inferred, and experienced. It is a catholic and open perspective.

Pepper affirms that *change* and *novelty* are "the ineradicable contextualist categories." Change and novelty occur, he says, as details within *quality* and *texture*. The latter may be said to be the working categories of contextualism. Under quality appear subheadings concerned with how an event (1) *spreads,* (2) *changes,* and (3) *fuses* (to some degree). Under texture we refer to a texture's (1) *strands,* (2) *context,* and (3) *references.* And under references it is noted that they may be (a) *linear,* (b) *convergent,* (c) *blocked,* and (d) *instrumental.* Says Pepper: "This system of concepts may be regarded as a set of working categories for handling the events of our epoch."[23]

Pepper states that quality and texture, the basic working categories, cannot be explained because of their categorical nature. They can only be shown or pointed to:

> . . . the quality of a given event is its intuited wholeness or total character; the texture is the details and relations which make up that character or quality.[24]

Qualities are central to our focus but do not constitute the focus of analysis. We proceed through analysis of the texture—the elements, features, details, and the like—but not at the expense of wholeness (quality). Thus quality and texture are not separable.[25]

There is not space to pursue further here Pepper's exposition of contextualism nor to criticize its method or its criteria of truth. (The latter task is reserved for the critique at the end of this book.) I did not seriously review Pepper's theory until the modes for this book were outlined in total and until half of them had been projected in discursive form. Yet I find that I have unknowingly, and perhaps unclearly, utilized many of his working categories. In particular, my reconstruction of expressive acts has paid attention to the detailing of "references" within the "strands" of "textures." Linear, convergent, blocked, and especially instrumental references have been discussed, but not called such. In the historical mode, for example, my intuitive emphasis (an arbitrary one, in that many other basic sets could be taken) on "concepts about art and making art held by the artist in the context of his drawing series" initiated a linear reference giving both direction and satisfaction to my search through the case material. A convergent reference was indicated by the similarity, again for example, of various concepts about making art found throughout the series. Also, concepts held by the artist about art and about making art interacted and converged (two different initiations for a linear reference eventuated in a common satisfaction, in Pepper's terminology). What Pepper calls blocking of a reference occurred, for example, when two different strands (concepts about making art in this case) crossed, as when Larry's two operations, one for texture and one for light and shade, became first confused (on the shoe drawing), then resolved in a novel way (for him, but in an explainable way by reference to the separate strands) through strokes indicative of light-shade and texture in the lines within the tree trunk. In Pepper's thinking, such an event could also be called an "integrative novelty" because "It is analyzable and understandable in retrospect but not predictable in its nature, nor in all its effects."[26]

In further detailing of the textures within a given event, we come to what Pepper calls "instrumental references." These bear closely upon blocking, referred to above. Much of what I observe and am given to share in the drawing lab comes under instrumental references. An original aim or movement of the artist is blocked and an instrumental episode, coherent in its own right, takes its position within the larger aim or movement.

> The result is often a texture of very extended and complicated integration. What holds it together is a linear reference that persists from lack of satisfaction. This is the positive dynamic factor in the integration. The negative factor is the blocking in the form of an intrusive novelty.[27]

By "instrusive novelty" Pepper means one for which one can account by attending to the past histories of crossing strands.[28]

What I am saying is that most of the novelties seen in my case studies of drawing are unpredictable but historically traceable occurrences related to blocking of operations (transformations) and to the interaction of dissonant conceptions about making art. Further, blocking in itself is of interest usually only to the degree that instrumental actions are undertaken as subordinate acts within larger episodes.

It is at this level that most change occurs, as I perceive it, although from time to time more severe shifts appear which are not only unpredictable but hard to trace as the result of blocked strands. Such, for example, was the shift that occurred between the fifth and seventh weeks of Larry's first term in the drawing lab (see pp. 45-52). If we allow for concepts about making art on several levels of abstraction, it may be possible to trace such a large change. Larry himself attributes it to the two very different avant-garde exhibitions he saw; he also mentions his depression even though making progress in solving representational problems; and we know that he and an art education major fell into serious and spirited discussion during the week-6 period in the lab, when no drawings were made. Still, it is harder in this instance to locate the instrumental reference and the blocking strands, except by speculating at a rather high level of abstraction.

In passing, I want to note that Pepper suggests how conquests of blocked references became part and parcel of larger directionality, as in the drawing series:

> . . . instrumental reference tends gradually to turn into articulated linear reference. Contextualists often make a great deal of this fact, . . . pointing out the dangers of conceiving the distinction of means and ends as absolute. An instrumental activity enters right into the texture of a terminal activity, and the structure of any complicated terminal activity is largely instrumental. . . . At the early stages of an instrumental act, when the obstacle is vividly felt, the instrumental activities are qualitatively taken as rather separate events, but as they become integrated with the terminal texture they fuse into the quality of one total texture.[29]

In passing to the larger perspective of the drawing series, we come upon an image of a kind of structure having continuity. I have already referred to my leanings toward a kind of organic cybernetics, where the artist is seen, abstractly, as a kind of "structure" of decidedly individual character. Piaget, in his book on *Structuralism,* provides the basic definition of a structure as "a systematic whole of self-regulating transformations."[30] Provided we are comfortable with a loose interpretation of "systematic" (at least in the sense of deriving the "laws" of the system from the individual case), I feel comfortable with such a structuralist cybernetics. Even more to the point is the way in which K. Buhler early indicated how structure can be seen from the "subjective" side, under the terms "intention" and "significance" (or meaning), which, again as Piaget reasons, are the counterparts, from the side of phenomenology, of "transformation" and "self-regulation" as the latter are employed on the side of the "objective" definition of structure.[31]

But does the world need to be so divided between "subjective" and "objective" structures? I think not. Transformations and self-regulation can be seen in the workings of an artist on the phenomenal level, but these are directly linked to intention and meaning within the existential view provided by the shared artist's stream of consciousness of the expressive act.

K. Buhler also distinguished between levels of complexity in thought in a way useful to our study of drawing. The first level is that of consciousness, which ascribes meaning; secondly, one is conscious of the rules which are involved in relational structures; and at the highest level of complexity, there is "the deliberate synthetic act 'intent upon' the construction of a whole, that is, a system of thought 'at work.'"[32] I believe these levels of complexity are discernible in the conceptualizations an artist constructs concerning his drawing processes. (They are much like the second- and third-order premises about making art earlier discussed.) Many of these concepts are formulated at the second level as the artist becomes conscious of his instrumental actions undertaken to remove his blocked satisfactions. The third level brings in those superordinate concepts that attempt to account for part-whole relations and qualitative fusions in the total textures of a drawing. Of such a nature, but still more complex, are those conceptualizations of the drawing series as a whole.

The focus on the drawing serial stresses the *genesis* of concepts about making art, thus removing one from static structuralist tendencies. This is true even though my own studies concentrate on the work of adults. By so doing I am properly concerned with *individual development* in art, and I would take such a view even were I working with young children. To paraphrase Piaget's genetic perspective on intelligence, it might be said that art concepts are the mirror of artistic work or thought in action—not the other way around.[33]

Textures can become extended—into chapters and books, into a drawing series, into the "serial" as we have used the term—and thus reach beyond the contextualist present. These can still be called textures, says Pepper,[34] but it is useful to call them "individual textures" to signify how they extend beyond more narrowly confined present events.

> In coming upon individual textures we are thus stepping out of the immediacy of present events into the evidence for a widely extended universe in which myriads of given events are interlocked and march forward arm in arm into the future with great strides.[35]

Individual textures, of which I identify the drawing serial as an excellent example, accrue from the concatenation of instrumental references. Larry's concepts about making art, spanning two and one-half years, give the conceptual fruits of instrumental references occurring in his extended series of drawings (see pp. 59-66), providing a complex and dynamic individual texture. We are thus carried out into larger textures, into the public as well as the private world, because "the context of a private texture is already some other texture, and the two textures are thus mutually conjoined and interpenetrating."[36] This brings us to our next mode.

Particular Theorizing Mode: The Type Concept

In chapter 2 I made reference to Arnheim's distinction between "type concepts" and "container concepts."[37] His argument was that perception often operates on goodness, clarity and unity of structure, upon the intuitive grasp of the exemplary form or case. Cognition, as usually conceived, however, proceeds, at least insofar as it must justify itself, by way of "container concepts" which are constructed by means of criteria which determine members allowable within the concept. If the reader will bear with me, I would like to use these distinctions as the base upon which to construct this and the following mode of inquiry.

Perhaps the distinction seems specious. I will attempt to show that there is a real difference between the two. The closer one sticks to the single case, the more he operates from a "type concept" base. The researcher cannot claim to "generalize" from a single case. Yet he leaves us with the distinct impression that he is telling us something about, in this setting, "drawing" in general. This occurs in much the same way that we learn something about "life" and its dynamics through the reading of a good biography or autobiography. First, as earlier discussion revealed, the biographer or autobiographer assumes some viewpoint toward his data which both limits his approach but at the same time makes meaning possible. He has symbolized and represented complex phenomena by the set evident in both his selection and interpretation of the events he takes as given. The insights we obtain are, of course, addressed toward the particular life in question, but since we as humans have much in common, we grasp in this unique life something of a "type" which informs us more broadly. I have decided to speak of these insights as "speculations" or "intuitions" rather than as "generalizations." (We will reserve the latter term for a more defined usage in the next section.) Perhaps such speculations are prelogical generalizations, a kind of tacit knowledge which cannot be easily shared or validated, but which generate the bases for later inquiry, yielding generalizations which can be logically defended. Thus, as in most of the modes of chapter 3, we gain insight by sympathy, by empathy, by reverberations, as it were. The only difference I feel is that the conceptualization of the "type" should be more consciously explicated. The prelogical "work" is pushed as far as possible. Certainly speculations arising from an exemplary case or type are "grounded" and, in that sense, are not just wild speculations. It is speculative thought that should be characterized by its fruitfulness for further inquiry. But in itself it is worthwhile. It is, at its best, a demonstration, a revelation.

The reader must forgive me for not giving a detailed example of this mode. In a way, Lowenfeld[38] and Schaefer-Simmern[39] present their case materials as "types" illustrative of their theories, and they not only speculate but generalize therefrom. Arnheim[40] does the same in a brief case presented as part of a more recent symposium. It may be a mere deceit, but I pride myself on more patience before the complexity of the intentional-functional behavior, covert and overt, which exists in the drawing process, conceived of as in the artist's hands and as occurring in a given situation. It is too early to do more than speculate. On the other hand, it may only mean that I do not have as clearly delineated a theory of art education as the authors referred to.

It would not be too difficult, however, to review the material on Larry under the historical mode of this chapter (pp. 59-63) with the intention of presenting him as a "type." This would take a still higher form of abstraction. I would speculate, for example, on how young adults of college age who are untrained in art (notice that I no longer refer to Larry but to a group whose parameters I am describing), who are in a self-instruction setting where they have an opportunity to review their processes and their feelings with interested and nurturant special observers over an extended time where the procedures remain constant, begin to try to master the representational skills they lack. They feel they cannot "express" anything prior to a certain level of such mastery. Simple devices are invented, combined, and varied, whether to catch the convention of perspective (converging lines, drawing of box-like figures, changing sizes, discovering the rudiments of atmosphere); to show projection via form demarcation (structural lines, as in face or torso); to show solidity by texture and light and shade. These devices, invented more in the classical experimental style—one variation at a time—interact to create complexity and the need for higher-order principles which unify the many elements. Often this occurs through a dependency on mood or pervasive feeling which, as the pieces are done, brings them under review for consistency.

The organization of complexity by controlling principles raises the whole issue of expression, for such feelings and moods as organize a whole unmistakenly emerge from the self and thus express that self to some degree. Complexity in a drawing also ushers in the variations of medium usage so that the physiognomic aspects of strokes, of speed, of texture, and the like, enter consciousness. Hand-medium-feeling connections focus attention on "process thinking."

Even so, until the beginner relaxes his fixation on illusionistic representation as an all-encompassing goal, he is in for frustration. Further, his way of working, while progresssing, is not sufficiently rewarding intrinsically. He achieves what he thinks he "should," but it does not stem from strong feeling, from desire.

In part, such an impasse is overcome through discarding the representational goal for the expressive goal, or at least in changing the value order of these. Connected with the expressive goal is one oriented toward the process "presence" of the drawing act itself. Expression and process-centering take priority over representational mastery (as an abstract goal overhonoring illusionistic realism.) The "in-here" interacts with and masters the "out-there." Further, if one looks at the art around one in the culture, especially the "high" art, it is concerned with much more than representation. In fact, in this century, it even gives up much concern with it, or at the least transgresses consciously against it.

Departures from realism lead one to prize abstraction and ambiguity for their expressive potential. One is surprised into meanings that seem to reside within visual phenomena and in the medium itself. One's confidence goes up as he feels secure enough to risk himself in the process of drawing itself. Confidence breeds a sense of identity and of patience—the belief that one's ability to create meaning will arise as he works. Continuity through repetition and extension, through discoveries out of the ground prepared (not out of nothing) in past drawings, allow one to abstract from a sense of identity how it is he works and what qualities have deep and lasting meaning for him. With this feeling of identity and continuity comes also a freedom to choose a new path, to explore, even to go against the path forming.

High-order abstractions about art and making art are now possible. Connections between art and life at their most intense continue to form, one feeding the other. One conceives what it is to be an artist and knows when he is an artist.

By reflecting again on Larry's case, I offer such speculations as those in the above paragraphs. These speculations present an abstraction concerning how untrained college-level beginners in drawing organically develop over an extended period of time, while working in a self-instructed, self-reflective, nurturant setting.

I have thus risked speculating about the dynamics of change in drawing from the in-depth focus provided by my phenomenological and contextual stance which permitted me indirect access to the artist's stream of consciousness as he guided himself through an extended drawing series. So doing is tantamount to claiming a kind of knowledge has been gained and that this can be shared. It can also be criticized in terms of its own logic and development; and it can be utilized toward other ends, as in sensitizing art teachers, or as the basis for generating hypotheses for further inquiry.

Other writers who work within a basically "clinical method," also present an individual case as though it is a type. They do this in several ways. Moustakas, for example, in writing on psychotherapy with children,[41] will present a case, with commentary preceding and following it, as though it exemplifies a category: the normal child, the disturbed child, the creative child, the handicapped child. Of course one might say that Moustakas had selected the cases he discusses out of a wealth of experience. While this is undoubtedly true, the problem still remains as to how the individual and the generic are represented simultaneously. Perhaps the prefatory and concluding remarks are meant to bear the burden of abstraction toward the generic. If so, we can only conclude that this is done in an informal and intuitive way out of the wisdom accruing from experience. The work of Coles is even more to the point. In *Children of Crisis* he utilizes drawings of children to gain insight into their values, attitudes, and perceptions on racial matters and on integration.[42] He admits to approaching these drawings clinically, from his perspective as a child psychiatrist. He says that he values what these drawings tell him of individual children, rather than what they say about children in general or about one or the other race.[43] Yet much that he finds he feels is shared between children as well, so that several pages from the above reference we find him saying:

> What have these children had to say in the drawings they have done these past years? Is there any reasonable way to categorize and classify their pictures so that the individual child's feelings are preserved, and yet more general conclusions made possible? I think the answer to the second question is yes, and I will try to show why by describing the interests and concerns these children reveal when they take up crayons or a brush.[44]

Grounded Abstract Theoretical Mode:
The Container Concept (Pooled Cases)

The fact that Moustakas and Coles vacillate between emphasis on the individual exclusively, on the individual as a type, and on the individual as a member of a category or class suggests how difficult it is to draw a line between the various modes presented. For the sake of conceptual clarity, I am trying to present the modes as distinct, but the astute reader will sense that they do indeed overlap.

If we start with an emphasis on the uniqueness of an individual case or centering on one expressive act, we are nevertheless inclined to situate our case in such a way that the spread from the private to the public texture, of which the contextualist speaks, occurs in the sense of speculations and intuitions about what we have learned about drawing in general. Sometimes this is a natural function of some larger set or perspective that we bring to all the material we present. This is true in Cole's book. He is not interested, for example, in the drawings as art expressions or as indicative of changes in drawing strategy and the like, but in the feelings children experience and express concerning racial relations. He visits the children in their homes, at school, and on the playground. He knows them over long periods of time. Thus he can establish a sufficiently rich and detailed context for interpretations or conclusions from the angle of his own perspective on the material. This is a perspective, moreover, which has determined much of the content of the drawings themselves. In this way, Coles operates from both a type and a container concept approach, although I read him as dealing more with the former. Actually, he does what he says: he honors the individual foremost, then he speculates according to his purposes and his speculations lead him to "more general conclusions" which still honor "the individual child's feelings."

Indeed, the case perspective in general commits one to a contextualist stance in which the actual historic events and their setting are accepted as of greatest value in inquiry. The method, as Pepper suggests, is synthetic and not analytical. It is no mistake that Coles speaks of *preserving the individual child's feeling* before anything else, or that Moustakas makes the case material largely speak for itself, adding only such commentary as extends it to the structure of his book concerned with children's psychotherapy. A pointing and a showing come first; then one can extend the sense of the qualitative wholeness of the material by exploration (notice that I find it had to say analysis) of the textures which are its structural components.

In this section I am trying to present what is essentially a pooled case history approach, in which containers or category concepts are involved. The individual thus becomes a member of a class, and therein lies the rub. Can the method here proceed as in medicine, where the records of those suffering from some malady are pooled and studied for abstractable commonalities of possible relevance to the malady? Could I take cases from the drawing lab and merge them to see what can be said about, for example, untrained college undergraduates working under self-instruction with special participant observers, stimulated recall and inquiry, and the like? Of course I could try various sortings of cases before such pooling—for example, cases where the students had no training but much exposure to art works and art ideas, as opposed to those lacking such exposure and concepts.

Such a method seems more oriented to hypothesis generation for later operational verification than the other modes discussed so far. By this I mean that categories or criteria for class membership so abstracted do not need to rely, later, on case histories at all. The criteria abstracted can be tested out on appropriate samples more directly, in the form of Barker's O-data. That is, structured interviews, observation schedules, tests and instruments intended to measure presence or absence, or degree of presence, of the abstracted properties can be constructed and applied. At this point, however, we have moved beyond the purpose and the restrictions set for this book and its modes.

In earlier days, I often began my study of drawings by a similar procedure. Drawings of a defined sample under defined conditions would be qualitatively examined by me and others for the purpose of educing criteria potentially descriptive of the set of drawings (usually in comparison with a set where other conditions obtained). Criteria so accumulated were then made into rating scales for application and validation upon a new set of comparable drawings to see whether the properties isolated indeed generalized.

By moving to such subsequent operations, formalizations, and instrumentations, however, we move from an idiographic to a nomothetic frame of reference, and from a contextualism honoring the agency of the artist (as "a systematic whole of self-regulating transformations" proceeding through implicit intentions and meanings which guide instrumental acts toward intrinsic satisfactions unique to given situations), to a reactive view where inputs and stimuli impinge upon a "black box" at best represented by explicit inferred intervening variables within the organism.

Thus the danger of a kind of reductionism injurious to the basic assumptions of this work arises rapidly in this mode, because much that is peculiar to the individual case is jettisoned in arriving at the pooled characteristics. The individual artist's feelings and intentions, the specific expressive act and its context, are not preserved. It is true, however, that feelings and intentions can themselves be made the subject of pooling, in which case it is the context from which they arise that is lost. By taking this route, we move perforce to an emphasis on abiding structures and away from the change and novelty I have argued are closer to the expressive act. Such semipermanent structures as concern us in art, I feel, gain their meaning within the individual lawfulness discernible in a given artist's series. Beyond that, speculations about drawing in general come better from the "type" than the "container" stance, under the basic assumptions of this book, even though I am resistant to "essences" which the type emphasis resurrects, if ever so subtly.

From the perspective of this book, the traditional hierarchy of modes is inverted, for the container concept idea moves away from vital data close to the artist's reconstruction of his stream of consciousness in the expressive act as shared by a special participant observer. It is thus on a lower order of value, even though on a high level of abstraction. The kind of abstraction involved cancels out the contextualist and idiosyncratic structuralist perspective compatible with our view of the making of art.

Still, there is nothing improper about proceeding according to this mode. "Better" and "worse" are labels only applicable to modes of inquiry from an explicit frame of reference. From my present frame of reference, this mode is reductive and less useful. But it is a coherent and consistent mode. I would even call this a "bridge mode," because it is here, if anywhere, that my basic contextualism (as tempered by a concern with the making of art from an existentialist, experiential base) could be sucked most easily toward what Pepper calls "mechanism." Mechanism rises

> as the stronger analytical and integrative theory, and contextualism as the stronger synthetic and dispersive theory. We are tempted to surmise that whatever system there is in the world is of the mechanistic type, and whatever dynamic vitality, of the contextualist sort.[45]

Thus an effort is made to wed a world hypothesis suffering from an "inadequacy of precision" to one suffering from an "inadequacy of scope." The one admits too little, the other too much.[46] But at bottom these views are incompatible. This mode underscores the problem, because at this point we will have to decide whether to weaken our brand of contextualism which preserves the unique, the concrete, the individual in all its richness, or to strengthen the side of explicit structure, precision, control, and public verification. No real merger is possible—only a master and slave relationship where some benefit is alleged to arise from the attempted association. The issue is a political one, not a philosophical one.

So, after pointing to the bridge and suggesting that one could make a valiant effort to preserve *more* of the individual case in entering the concept mode, I must nevertheless admit that my inclination is to turn my back on this mode. It does not lead to a promised land, but to a different land altogether. I was there, and I can return if I wish. The landscape on this side seems structurally more similar to art as I experience it. This book is about the geography of the region on this side of the bridge.

Formative Hermeneutic Mode in the Individual Setting

Before this point, I have acknowledged that the participatory conditions of inquiry compatible with my assumptions have in themselves interacted with the phenomena under study. But this effect has been unavoidable. Without the interaction, the sharing and appreciation of the artist's actions, thoughts and feelings are not accessible. The interactive element up to now, however, has been instrumental and not deliberate.

It is possible to more consciously interact with the artist in an effort to comprehend him. In this mode, as in spirit in the earlier concept of action research or in the present notion of formative (as opposed to summative) evaluation, ongoing "treatments," "measurements," and the like, are introduced in an effort to comprehend the dynamics of change within the system under study. In the context of this book, historical and aesthetic interpretation related to the individual artist's case would be pragmatically enjoined to the furtherance of the artistic serial (the string of expressive situations). This mode thus goes beyond sharing, empathy, and waiting to conscious participation via interpretation attached to feedback and reflective inquiry into the ongoing artistic serial.

The term "formative," as suggested, refers to the in-process application of the mode under discussion. It takes on, thus, the connotation of an action which intervenes or intrudes in a quasi-experimental way. As I hope to show, however, there are safeguards which tone down such meanings considerably. *Hermeneutics* is defined as "the science of interpretation and explanation, especially that branch of theology which defines the laws whereby the meaning of the scriptures is to be ascertained." *Hermeneutic* means, then, "unfolding the signification; interpretative; as *hermeneutic* theology."[47]

The psychologist Jung speaks of "hermeneutic treatment" in his discussion of the dream series. It was his discussion which led to conceptualization of this mode. He says:

> Hermeneutic treatment of imaginative ideas leads to the synthesis of the individual and the collective psyche. . . . As soon as ever we begin to map out the lines of advance that are symbolically indicated, the patient must begin to proceed along them. . . . He is in truth obliged to take the way of individual life which is revealed to him, and to persist in it until and unless an unmistakable reaction from his unconscious warns him that he is on the wrong track.[48]

The method whereby this is done is also spelled out by Jung. The explanatory method ". . . consists in making successive additions of other analogies to the analogy given in the symbol."[49] Apparently the first analogy or interpretation is to be given by the patient himself, in a kind of work of active imagination in his own behalf. Then the analyst and patient together search for objective analogies in various cultural fields and in the history of symbols and archetypes. He says:

Even the best attempts at explanation are only more or less successful translations into another metaphorical language . . . the most we can do is to dream the myth onwards and give it a modern dress.[50]

The key phrases from Jung refer to "the synthesis of the individual and collective psyche" which is brought about through "making successive additions of other analogies to the analogy given in the symbol" so that the individual can "dream the myth onward." The symbol is looked upon by Jung from a pragmatic and existential stance. Its meaningfulness is dependent upon the attitude of the interpreting consciousness.

In this stance we can envision intervening in the artist's behalf so that his frame of reference is kept expansive, flexible and open, but never oriented away from his own base in experience and meaning. Thus the culture is not mediated willy-nilly to the artist, but new conceptualizations and symbolizations in keeping with his experiential base are explored to see whether they help him "dream the myth onwards." If such explorations are not helpful, the artist will say so, or his series will warn him that "he is on the wrong track."

From my own position, but not yet from my studies in a consistent way, I would predict that the most useful formative hermeneutic focus would be one which consciously constructed organizational concepts and relational concepts about making art abstracted, under the artist's lead, from his own series and his reflections thereon. Such concepts as Larry developed (summarized in brief on p. 53) would be an excellent base for extending his frame of reference by "making successive additions of other analogies" to those given in his own interpretations. The test of success is a simple one: the additions would fall into the service of meaning, they would extend Larry's aesthetic encounter into more depth.

My defense of this mode as one of inquiry is that it intensifies the artist's serial through its *active* nurturant frame, rather than operating from a more passive, counter-interventionist nurturant frame, but that it does not intend to deflect the artist's course any more than the more passive, "actively"-waiting posture. The lead is still the artist's, even though there is an active effort to help him focus more intensely on the meaning and direction of his own series. It is as though the participant observer, in his special role, can accommodate the culture to the artist in a way that he might assimilate it, or at least interact with it toward his own ends. In terms of knowledge and appreciation of the artist's serial, the participant observer gains insight into how the artist interacts with specific intrusions, interpretations, and conceptualizations about art. There is an interface between the private, and the public, between the individual and the collective psyche.

But I will not be able to speak with any assurance of this mode until I have felt its operation directly. Currently in the drawing lab the only formative hermeneutic effect discernible is in the focusing, connective, and restatement function presently at work, where the special participant observer takes his cue from the artist's own reflections and from his history of statements and helps to bring these to clarity in the artist's consciousness. My own temperament and the working ethic of the lab up to now incline me toward the more passive role. But if a formative hermeneutic mode can remain sensitive to the artist's personal causation, idiosyncratic meaning, and intentional symbolization, can honor the artist's effort to reconstruct his active role in expression, then it might also speed up and highlight our grasp of an individualistic "systematic whole of self-regulating transformations." I hesitate, too, because it would seem that O-data will thus intrude upon our T-data and what I have called D-data, or that my role would change from one of nurturing-knowing to nurturing-teaching. My own intuition is that more artistic learning and knowledge acquisition are possible within the nurturing-knowing stance presently in effect.

Spread, Fusion, and Integration The Description of the Artist's Superordinate Concepts on the Making of Art

5

Readers intent on what I am saying on alternative modes of research may wish to skip this chapter, for here I want to take an interlude to discuss conceptualizations that artists hold about their art which are highly abstract and metaphorical. They are, in fact, close to "individual myths." They do not arise, as a rule, all of a sudden; and they often persist, in a motivational sense, over great periods of time—even for an artistic lifetime. The in-depth study of an artist and his artistic serial grants us the ground on which to cognize the form, growth, and possible meaning of the idiosyncratic artistic myth, as I will call it for want of a better label.

I intrude this topic at this point to balance the superficial and partly reductive effect of concentrating solely on modes of interpretation and description. If this book were on one or two artists and not concerned with exploring alternative modes of inquiry into the making of art, then such superordinate concepts or idiosyncratic artistic myths as here discussed in brief would arise naturally, I believe.

It is apparent that I attach great meaning to the organizing and directing cognitive structures of the individual artist. But I would not want to suggest that the artist somehow "thinks up" these highly abstract concepts or artistic "philosophies" consciously, deliberately, or quickly—though indeed artists will differ in this as in all else. Such synthesizing ideas usually have a long history. They may indeed go back into childhood, but they may as well be a slowly-acquired world outlook. In either case, it is their directing and guiding power in the present which is our topic.

Whatever is in mental life becomes the raw material for fusion with artistic causality, idiosyncratic meaning, and intentional symbolization. More than that, it interfuses with tool, medium, and image directly. Yet I acknowledge the limit suggested by Malraux when he said that the artist may say what he pleases, but in practice he will paint only what he can.[1] My own inclination, as later examples may show, is perhaps to overplay the literary aspect of the higher-order conceptualizations under discussion. Be that as it may, it is clear that I will need some kind of evidence from the artist himself to guard against my own tendency to read into the serial what may not really be there. For this, written fragments from personal documents (letters, diaries, poems, and the like) and recorded interview materials are the readiest documentation. I will attempt to draw upon both.

I will take a transactional and genetic view toward the idiosyncratic artistic myth. By this I mean that existing cognitive "structures" are the raw material which interacts with the ongoing artistic serial. The latter draws upon this conceptual material but transforms and shapes it in doing so. All that is in the mind cannot be linked to the drawing, but what is in the mind becomes the base for decisions which have to do with the symbolic transformation of feedback from the specific drawing itself. This is logical if we remember the link between intention and meaning (the subjective equivalent of transformation and self-regulation). It is not necessary to get caught between essentialism and existentialism in this issue. My position is merely that mental structures enter into the expressive situation and are both influential and changed therein. (I would, if pressed, side with Sartre's famous statement that existence precedes essence, particularly where we talk of art expression.)

An example of what I refer to can be found in Milner's book, *On Not Being Able to Paint*.[2] Milner describes how she had to learn that in art one did not work under tight conscious control, from purpose to deed. Rather, as in the case of Larry (used for many examples in chap. 3 and 4) and others in the drawing lab, she had to learn to give herself up more to the art process itself, allowing her feelings, vague as they might be, and the concrete explorations in the changing drawing to guide her. So she gradually learned to do "free drawings" in which the dialogue nature of the expressive act takes over (she calls this the method of "reciprocity"). As with Larry, she learns to conceptualize her own drawing strategies and the qualities emerging in her series. She talks, however, about her drawings according to the symbolic overtones and latent content they reveal. And here, as one might suspect, since she is a psychoanalyst, the meanings which she finds relate to psychoanalysis on the one hand, and to psychic creativity on the other. It is to her credit, however, that she reserves her technical analytical explorations for an appendix. The rest of the book is closer to the actions and feelings of drawing itself. I venture to say, though, that her drift to certain fantasies and symbolic content owes as much to the mental structures she takes to the act of drawing as to those she discovers and brings away. This is only natural, and so saying I do not at all detract from the fact that the meanings of her "free" drawings are forged in action (or in interaction.)

That the drawing process itself exercises strong influences upon intention and imagination, even when one is not completely process-centered or engaged in a "free" drawing, is suggested in the following reflection from an untrained artist working in our drawing lab:

> I like to draw from imagination. I've done this for some time. Imagination is drawing what you want to see. When there's a model right in front of you, you can't do this. It directs you, and you forget what you want to see. Imagination will correct for what you can't do, because you know whether you can do it, or change it to what you can do. You have to make a compromise.

This same girl later revealed that she had gone through three phases in the thirty weeks she spent in the drawing lab. (These occurred in three separate ten-week periods spread over two years.) At first she told the brush what to do; then she let the process and the brush interact with her desires—sometimes the process took the lead, sometimes she did, but it passed back and forth; finally, the drawing took on a genuine autonomy of its own, almost as though it painted itself—it flowed through her as a fused and integrated whole.

Another girl, an art major, had the opposite kind of problem. She was consciously trying to be "spontaneous" and produced one "organic abstract" after another. At the end of her ten-week session in the drawing lab the following exchange took place between us as we reviewed forty-five of her drawings. (*B* is the author, *D* is the artist.)

B. At first the drawings seem both more complex and more confused.

D. That's a good word. I never know what I'm doing, but I later felt more control. Like I can direct myself. The brush wouldn't take me. I'd take the brush and move it. At first I didn't know what I was doing, but I also didn't know what I was *going* to do.

B. How's that?

D. I knew the process I was going through but I didn't know the product that was coming. The first ones are more like sections of something bigger. The end ones are more separate, complete in themselves.

These contrasting examples are meant to illustrate that there is no one continuum or hierarchy of concepts about how to do one's art apart from the individual case or context under review. Beginners often do move toward freeing their intentions and preconceived images within the drawing process itself, but a more experienced artist may just as easily feel the need for greater structure and control within the dynamics of medium-image-feeling-process.

If the reader refers to Larry's conceptualizations about making art (summarized on p. 63), he will see that especially the last nine "points" listed (nos. 18-26) begin to fuse into an acquired world-outlook related to art. Here the synthesis is difficult and complex. Consider, however, an artist who can consciously theorize about his drawing strategies and the qualities of his successful works, who sees himself as an artist and the drawing process as a live encounter, where emotion is translated into "purely visual" terms. Maybe I should let Larry speak for himself:

> To get any kind of a point. . . . I have certain things that I want to do. . . . Well, it's as much discovery, you know, as it is control. But, you know, I have something that I want to get out, and if I don't get it out, it doesn't have any real relationship to what I did before and what I do next. . . . The visual sense . . . I don't know if you can develop it or not. I think [laughs] I've been having a hard time. I don't know whether I've gotten anywhere or not. . . . The visual sense, that's the medium you're working with, and in the expression of the emotions, as Collingwood says, these emotions have to be visual . . . maybe tactile.

Here, interestingly, we see how Larry has been able to assimilate influences from a philosophy course directly into his drawing experience. He had talked of the "visual sense" before his contact with Collingwood, but the latter helped him tie scattered ideas together. In the inquiry on his "Baltimore drawing" (pp. 69-75) Larry said:

> It's like, maybe, if you can just be struck with something but not really consider— Collingwood says "define your emotion"—I don't know if that's exactly it, but it's something like that. I don't have words. . . . It's like, if you're drawing it, like, the visual thing and the emotional impact that you feel, you kind of consider it more than if you just kind of keep it in your mind. Maybe I'd be just struck by this scene. I'd say I'd be a lot more aware of the scene and of my feelings after doing it.

Such examples as these direct our attention to the development of what I have called superordinate concepts on the making of art or the idiosyncratic artistic myth. Certainly an individual texture emerges as we examine the qualitative fusion or integration of concepts that arise above an artist's series, spreading backwards and forwards from the present. The conscious verbalization of these integrated concepts may or may not occur. In my opinion, it never occurs early in a drawing serial. It emerges through the convergence of separate strands of meanings and process discoveries, of solutions to blocks and failures, and through the slow grasp of qualitative features of successful wholes.

If I had material of still more scope and depth, I could more easily illustrate the nature of the topic under discussion. It requires almost a life perspective. If the reader is game, I intend to turn to material from my own earlier drawings. In so doing, I depart from a principle on which I usually operate which maintains that it is difficult to make oneself an object of study. I say this because of the resultant confusion of roles between, for example, doing art and cognizing how one does art. Or, to take another example, I find it next to impossible to do any "content analysis" of the inquiry transcriptions from the drawing lab. I am in those dialogues so directly that I lack distance when it comes to analysis. I would willingly yield them up to some other observer for analysis. As it is, they constitute a transparent medium through which I cognize how another artist does his art. True, I develop higher-order conceptualizations about how I act in this context. But these concepts guide me and keep me responsive and sensitive. Perhaps with enough passage of time, I will be able to look *at* these dialogues, not *through* them to something else.

The drawings to which I refer are from twenty to thirty years old, for the most part, so that I feel less involved in them in an ego-defensive way. Even so, I will do no more than hint at the idiosyncratic artistic myth which surrounds them and arises from them. Further, there are some written personal documents, of a diary or quasi-literary nature, which give further insights into our topic. The written statements were done in the "middle," not the "early" period. This I find instructive of itself, for it suggests that the conscious need to verbalize came *after* the myth was underway, and that it came in a kind of semi-poetic form attempting to parallel the visual and artistic experiences from which it developed. Also, these drawings and writings were not done for the end of knowledge, in even a semi-conscious sense, but for expressive and commemorative ends.

Space will allow me to present only a small portion of this material. What I select is not chosen for its artistic merit, but to round out examples of highly abstract concepts about making art. Illustrations will refer to an early period (1940-46), a middle period (1947-55), and a later period (1956-65). The written documents belong to the middle period (1947-55). I will present two kinds of idiosyncratic artistic myths which, while related, can be discussed somewhat independently. The first I will label the "Bach-music landscape theme," the second merely "the river theme." The first theme occurs near the end of the early period (World War II years), whereas the river theme precedes and outdates the earliest and latest time series (I still draw upon it, for example, in decorating pottery).

The setting for the Bach-music landscape theme I will try to construct as briefly as possible. I grew up as the middle of three boys in a minister's family. Of a religious and somewhat introverted temperament, I early responded to nature in, at first, an animistic, then a pantheistic manner. Organic processes, especially as experienced in the midst of landscapes in solitude, exemplified the ultimate mysteries and powers to me. My own perception, caught in the flux of time and experience, seemed bursting with meaning and the need to capture and express that meaning and presence I felt. Animate and inanimate forms had gestures, and they were not separated entities, but parts of organic wholes. When I sketched anything, I tried to catch this vague (in verbal expression) but very real feeling.

My serious drawing and painting began in mid-adolescence. It was a private and seclusive inner world, but it was allowed and even passively nurtured (if not understood) by those around me. Actually, my behavior was not that far removed from "religious experience," although I felt ambivalent toward institutional forms of the latter, while retaining my respect for my parents' involvement in them and for my own private notion of religion.

The organic and fused feeling of music was a central part of my inner world, and I lived a steady diet of classical music. More than once I detected equivalences of structure between certain music and certain feelings I struggled to express in painting and drawing. Eventually I became totally enamored of the music of Johann Sebastian Bach. This is a powerful identification that persists even now. He is the only composer I do not tire of, it seems.

To shorten the account let me say that gradually my feeling for some of the baroque characteristics of Bach's music began to permeate my perception of certain landscapes. The latter were usually those with a multiplicity of elements which seemed to be caught up in the rhythm of a whole scene. I took to trying to capture this integrated musical visual feeling in direct drawing from nature. Thirty years later, I can talk of this. At the time, you can be sure I kept it to myself for the most part.

I do not mean that I *heard* Bach-like music while in the presence of the landscape and while drawing it on-the-spot. Rather there was a transposition or paralleling of feeling, an equivalence of structure, which guided me. It was never a matter of saying "this is such-and-such a (Bach) piece in landscape form." It was more abstract than that. That's why I refer to it as an idiosyncratic artistic myth. It was metaphorical and magical, that is, but at the same time I *lived* it. It was, to borrow from Jung, a myth that I tried to dream onwards.

In figure 10 is shown such a landscape effort. This was drawn at the time I entered the European theater of war action during World War II. I was in an infantry rifle company which landed in France via Marseilles, so that we encamped in the land of Cézanne and Van Gogh. (The drawing, in fact, is of Mt. Ste. Victoire.)

Figure 10. Bach-music landscape

Figure 11 shows a similar landscape, but in this case the effort is carried beyond the on-the-spot conquest of the "music." Here, using pen and ink and simple water-color washes, the initial sketch is pushed to what I considered the full musical effect. Technically, I used a curious fattening of upsurging (aspiring) small curved elements. This treatment is one that developed over a number of drawings. It was laid directly on top of the on-the-spot sketch (such as fig. 10, in which there is just the slightest accent on the upward-moving curves).

I am not concerned here with artistic quality, but with the genesis of concepts like these. Consider that the case in point has its experiential and conceptual origins, and that it took a considerable period of time for these to become synthesized into one large point of view.

The Bach-music landscape theme more or less ended at the close of World War II. I remember developing a painting along these lines, using heavy blacks and bright translucent colors on a gesso ground, which was viciously torn apart by one of my college painting teachers. It was, she said, "unpainterly, stereotyped—I can't stand to look at it." You can be sure that I have a vivid memory of this incident.

The river theme has a longer history. The Bach-music landscape theme is actually superimposed upon this larger theme. In one way, the musical theme has its

Figure 11.   Bach-music landscape

clear formal aspect, whereas the river theme does not. It, more likely, has its very potent semantic and symbolic aspect, which it gets from a time stretching back still farther than the musical theme. Since the age of six, I lived close to the Susquehanna River in Harrisburg, Pennsylvania, when the "River Road" was not (at first, at least) a main highway route, so that the tree-lined approaches, the widely expanding vistas, the stately homes and broad grounds were unhurried and fused with nature. I walked along this river almost daily. I saw it in all seasons, in all kinds of weathers, at all times of the day. I was there on Sundays when people dressed up and took a walk; or on Easter when the "parade" formed with people in their new finery, converging on the "Sunken Garden" where the Japanese cherries and spring flowers were often in bloom. I was there during the lonelier workaday times when it was nearly deserted. I saw the lovers, the playing children, the bicyclers, the dog-walkers, the mothers with their babies, and the very old. It was a setting signifying life, but a kind of public-private, semi-institutional life occurring upon a spectacular natural stage. It was a blend of the limited and the free,

Figure 12.   River theme

of the real and the ideal. It became a focus through which I thought I could see all of life, but see it somehow as unified within a bigger perspective or within larger forces. The parallels again to religious and artistic experience will be obvious to many readers. Above all, it signified the passing of time with form and continuity, without the severe ruptures rendering one moment discontinuous with the next—the latter, characteristic of much of life, it seemed to me.

Along this route I made literally hundreds of drawings. Sometimes these were carefully done. At other times they were scrawled in quick strokes on envelopes, parts of paper bags, and the like. In figure 12 are shown three early sketches. The first is a more faithful rendering of a scene. This is followed by a semi-abstract schematic representation of the same scene which tries to catch something of the structure and gesture sacrificed in the more careful drawing. The third is similar to the second, but still more broadly laid in. In the second sketch I scrawled in these words as well:

> Non-intense sky (less intense than leaves)—All blue, river and sky—all warm street, pavement and greens—street and pavement a near gray (warm) to sky value—feeling of a structure—feeling of blues of sky as isolates or of stained glass—middle trees penetrate through the structure.

On the third sketch I wrote:

> Green and black (even sun green is dark), vs. cream and tan (sidewalk) and blue (river, sky and distance).

Thus through visual detail, simplified structure, and notes couched in words close to painting cues, I hoped to catch a specific time and feeling and a general structure or continuity.

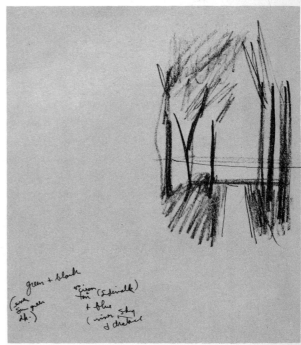

In figure 13, also from the early period, are shown two on-the-spot sketches which attempt to catch life in context. The first is one of many pen and pencil sketches of the "sunken garden" by the river, with suggestions of people in place. The second attempts to capture an older man sitting on a bench and talking with a woman, while his three small dogs (repeated several times) romp around beside them. After all these years (thirty) I still see the color, life, and distance this was to recall.

Many times I took my on-the-spot sketches and semi-abstract on-the-spot schemas and carried them into carefully executed "finished" drawings. Most of these were done when I was away from home and river—for example, during my years in the army in World War II. Figure 14 illustrates such a drawing.

Figure 13. River theme (p. 94)

Figure 14. River theme (below)

In this early period, I also made semi-abstract "finished" drawings. Figure 15, for example, takes this approach and conceives of the arching trees as echoing church architecture. There is the suggestion of sanctifying the place and its activities, and thus, for me at least, the connection between my earlier feelings about religion and nature. Undoubtedly, such drawings have much more meaning for me than they will for the casual observer. The latter will see, however, that there is some connection in style between figure 15 and slightly later drawings in the Bach-music landscape series (figure 11).

The river theme remains persistent. In figure 16 is shown a series of semi-abstract theme and variations sketches of one river motif. Figure 17 illustrates a still more formalized manipulation of river theme elements, here related to thoughts of pottery decorations. These examples come from the later period (roughly ten years ago).

In the eight illustrations shown (figs. 10 to 17), then, one can see examples of the kinds of drawings I did relating to two continuing themes. These span, as I

Figure 15.   River theme (below)

Figure 16.   River theme (p. 97, top).

Figure 17.   River theme (p. 97, bottom).

have indicated, about twenty-five years (1940-65). They symbolize an array of meanings which together constitute what I have called something close to an idio-syncratic myth. Stylistic and formal characteristics are shaped by such a pervasive world-view, for in-process transformations are guided by means of the funded meanings and feelings arranged in depth therein. Perhaps I use myself as an example because I know what I have kept secret over such a long time, and I lack ready material from the artists I have studied. For one thing, I have seen the artists in the drawing lab within a purposely bounded context, and over a relatively short span of time (up to thirty "producing" weeks spread over two and one-half years).

What are some other signs of the idiosyncratic myth and of superordinate concepts about making art? In my own case, there are writings. These, as I indicated earlier came during the middle period (1947-55), after the drawings were well under way. I am a little self-conscious about sharing these, but I know no other way to get into this issue. The fragments are often semi-poetic in intent. Like the sketches, they were often done on-the-spot. If they became actual poems, they were re-worked away from where they were begun, much like the finished drawings. They were, unfortunately, undated (except for the more finished poems), so that I can only roughly place them within the nine-year period indicated. Sometimes they were on scraps of paper which were carried around in my pocket or wallet (with resultant torn or obliterated parts). Sometimes they are interspersed with sketches. My plan here is to present a sampling of these in what I believe is their chrono-logical order (although I cannot usually give a precise date). Except for the one poem, what follows are fragments.

Fragment 1:

In walking down here to the River, I noticed that the smallest thing, the most ungainly twig or bush or pitiful porch step, was not in fact ill-designed as our train-ing may have tried to suggest, but possessed of a larger unity the whole of which was not a mere summation of its parts. This configuration, my spring (for my con-sciousness in this time and place are also mere elements of the total), rules all. And the two boys riding by me on their bicycles, against the River, mentioning an atom bomb in a ship and the like, are myself of twenty years ago, and more resemble me than differ by their different subject matter. They did not heed me one bit.

The poem I began to compose on the way down has gone into this. And I must walk on to the Sunken Garden. A glimpse up an alley-way from the River was moving indeed, with its banded shadows, depth and varied life and renewed variation on a theme that my eyes must always hear. A dog, and a girl on a bicycle moved slowly, attached to a solid band of shadow.

Fragment 2 (each of these fragments is a different occasion):

A bench, a hedge, a white glass globe, a parent shadow and a vernal splatter on the sky; notched weathered wood beneath my seat; pure color's passion and pure sky's blent blue and green. And I am all upon my eye, my eye is all upon this green, this scene, this theme.

This is a garden many times my own; sunken, yielding into earth to give to river's plane its perfect ground. This is an ideal place unreal—a patch, infinitesi-mal, a reference point for other shore, and River's edge, for life, for love and age; for children, for derelicts and fashion's girls—for many and for none, for present and for past.

Fragment 3:

A white cherry, darker-more-intense than turgid water's moving plane; a blos-som's snow of flight through air and path aligned.

The far shore leans more clearly toward the heart, and pits itself against the watery break of distance and of mind. The light more dazzles there—the hills drop off on unknown thoughts.

Fragment 4 (Easter morning):

I am so full of life and song that I can make no use, but live. These lonely quiet things, all moving in change, yet stable against the time of people and my own small tragedy of unfulfillment—these are my solid part. When shadows netted on the ground lose origin of sun and obstruction, and like spontaneous pigment from a modern thing just "are," my joy is not undone. It presses me, the lack of many things, but not this one direct and truthful cry at littlest bud, at light, at distance—at anything I do not ever know that leaves me free.

The lights of windows over River become mere playful sparks that form innumerably anew. The shadows loosely lie along the structured street, whose rigid immobility steps back for the aimless living movement of a few people placed as if for composition's sake. All chance things now form a higher order, seen against this transformed monotony, where light and shade and season cancel all complaints. So River, tree, window, yard, well known, become the background for my chance delight. Like this, that chilling wind near warmth of spring, that cloud of white across the water plane, that sound of bell, that girl in spreading tan spring outfit, all completed . . .

Some people come to walk their dog, some for habit or no clear reason—I, to walk my mind, to stalk my past and future.

Fragment 5:

In my eagerness to share my insights with others I forget the rarity and value they possess for me purely because of the context in which they occur within my own life. That idea which now fascinates me so much, does so precisely because of what I had thought on the matter before, or because of a dissatisfaction I might have had when I tried to resolve it. While the importance I ascribe to my new idea enables me to tell it with conviction and sincerity, yet it cannot occupy the place for another that it did for me.

Then, as a teacher, what more can I do than hold back enough that, within the context or interior landscape of my students, there will be a chance for rare and valuable insights to occur? Usually I will not see what these are, for one's landscapes are rarely revealed to another.

Fragment 6 (poem, a fragment):

> Those secondary sedimentary clays
> Wash down smelling of long ways and weather,
> Slow repositories of slower energies,
> They take on fuller hues from fire
> By virtue of impurities.
>
> The lines lie flat upon my river there,
> They form the sign of current and obstruction
> > down below,
> And there the pure reflection and dark shore
> Compose a still, delicious deep I cannot
> > comprehend or use at all.
>
> > (July 1955)

Fragment 7 (poem, River Road):

> The river road!
> A trappean catapult to space,
> Of temple trunks and oaken traves,
> Cross thicket-thatched to gloried sky.
>
> A present immemorial wind
> Plays over hedge and balustrades
> To floating transoms of the mighty nave.
>
> Within that timeless lonely place
> I hear intoned the long shore's song,
> And suffer on the past.

The wheel of evening runs the far hill's rim,
Sinks, and is gone.
It throws a senseless afterglow
On frantic unseen trees
And leaves inquietude of mind to me.

Oh, how spring air did warm this winter morn,
When richly underpainted fields
Shone on the dazzling ice-flowed river,
And lonely streets of distance shook
With plain songs and chorales.

A fearful immortality flows by:
A sweet confluence—
Then with now,
Self with river.

(Winter 1955)

Fragment 8:

An image burned into the mind is not a transparent color slide, because the former is capable of infinite projections upon the screen of the mind in the darkened room of the past-in-the-present. Visual elements are there, but they are pure spirit. I recall yesterday the banquet which my class spread out on a damp, enclosed path, within a cavern of tangled rhododendron, between two virgin hemlocks, around each of which the path circled, as though for awe or dance. There was too much food, possibly, since the meal was not planned in any detail or foreknowledge. Everyone brought something and we combined it. I did not expect it to look any certain way. I did not know where supplies and people would fall out along the path. Very little was fore-ordained. The selective nature of my own perception was unconsciously at work there, as retained images now tell me. But my greatest image is a fused one of sight and smell and taste and sound and observation and sensation. It is partly the damp earth on which I sat, on which I later lay and from which I saw cloud forms on an oval screen of blue through the depth of infinite layers of leaves and circular vaults progressively leading one upward in steps to the thrust above. It is partly a folk tune or two I was relaxed enough to sing or hum, with the memory of other voices joining in. Whose voices I am not sure, but their heads were near mine in some instances, across the path in others. My image of this comes at once, but in no set combination; yet it has combined all of the descriptive elements above, and more, and a series of times, into one.

My home and love, music, art, poetry are like this. But perhaps the river is more a symbol for this fusion within me than any other. "The river" does not even have a name to me. "The Susquehanna" is something else. This river is more the river of my experience of everything, since around it, as core, as unspeakable symbol, it organizes all else. It is a perpetual point of reference in my history. It merges into infinite echoes and images more things and meanings than the forest banquet raised to the tenth power—and I did not even begin to probe that banquet.

Fragment 9:

It strikes me I know nothing more beautiful than this river. It does not say the past. I walking here. It does not say anything. Therein lies its endless mystery and appeal. It is unfinished, imperfect—needing the completion of myself, my past, my imagination, a certain day and light, a certain cost at which I come to see it—as stealing away from table and loved ones, or too easy pleasures.

This purest blue of distance, this sun-filled trunk, these structured trees, this green transcendent, and that flash of sun and flesh—a fish in nature's water. Here all is light, and nothing old, though you may antique it in the trial.

What magnetism draws me here? A place so public is most private. A private wood is most public. Do all excellences depend in part on disappearance, on contradiction? It took me a full quarter hour to decide, standing on the corner where I came upon the river, whether to go down the river or up. I went up—more like a live fish. The cars and people, all a-color, move in and out amid this unity. No shadow out of place, no forced design, and yet more than I see, having so completely seen, so often felt.

In any piece of nature all colors lie suspended—all relations. Structure, light and shade, and color—hover 'round the perceiving brain. Modern, classic, romantic—all.

We all come down and wander along here dreamily. Especially on holidays—as though we have knowledge that life is meant for something better than we taste, as though by this symbolic act we may at least register what side we're on—or would be—before we return to the life that needs something better. We all as dumbly, but less peaceably, take our other courses.

The late glow on balustraded porch burns like a phrase, or like the loved one near. Closer harmonies are matters of the intellect. This time of day remains "my light"—corny by modern standards, or at least Venetian, it is the light of autumns and of late afternoons, warm, slanting, banding long shadows; and is like the squares of colored glass around the windows in my parents' old house, which first showed me, under feeling, that things change when seen under slightly changed conditions.

I see all knit together—even of this poorer stuff. But only I can take this cloth from off this loom. You can't see anything from the car anymore than, say, what special piece of cloth you'd like from going through a textile mill. I passed a long dark puddle again, which lit up with sky, late sun on porch, and dark inverted dome of trees.

My early things had truth—the truth of action, of aspects of reality torn from the living body of nature. Let my later have power, as harder won, more precious. A flame, I've seen, is kept with scraps of wood; and little twigs burn brightest, hottest—the humblest of wood. They need, however, continual attention.

When I come home I don't think in the present only, but in a thousand times through it. This makes for work, for I have a mind that would make a bread of everything.

My father's spirituality in me was driven underground; my mother's personal love became impersonal.

The river dances and shimmers; its infinitesimal sparks go on and off by thousands. And nature's feeling is of multiplicity and unity. Here (across the river) one has the distance that is needed for contemplation. The incomprehensibility of the real (perception) far transcends our fantasies. There is always an air and movement here. A man walks through shadow stripes and gapes. The near trees are architectural, the distance poetic, the cars black beetles with high gloss. The lights, the neutrals, are the river, the street and pavement, the sky. The sun-drenched arbor, the cloud-strewn street.

A near tree, on the bank, in the sun, flung against the river's and the sky's distance, is a considerable thing, not to be outdone by color slide or abstract art. A merest small cloud there—the tree an imperfect individual.

In nature nothing's filthy (not even the dog shitting on the green while the lady attending stupidly looks and waits—what a symbol for her days along the river!). Here nothing is honored, no station matters—and so all is honored, as all stations. Except sometimes my spittle sours a bit—a fault of the flesh, and not the sun.

Fragment 10:

Times and places are inextricably bound together, and their tie is often based on the flimsiest or most erratic of associations, or the most subjective and even subconscious of motivations. The truth of an interplay of lights and shadows upon forms of seeming stability, is that the instability and changes of these seemingly solid forms—changes in nature and in ourselves and in the very structure of each, changes of the real and the abstract, the fantastic and the formal, the past and the present, modern and traditional, material and mystical, the possible and the ineffable—all of these paradoxes are expressible through an active interplay of light and shade itself, without sharing in the highly arbitrary character of much modern art and life.

Of the ten fragments given above, in their order in time as well as I can establish it, some (fragments 1, 2, 3, 4, and 9) were done on-the-spot; some (fragments

6 and 7) were done in place and then worked upon again later; and some fragments 5, 8 and 10) were delayed reflections, away from the river.

As with the drawings of my own (figs. 10 to 17), the written fragments are not presented for qualitative appraisal (in fact, their wording embarrasses me) but rather as an example of a system of complex cognitive constructs operating on art, memory, and perception. I have called such complexes idiosyncratic artistic myths. I wish to underline their dynamic character—the fact that they are transformed and extended even as they operate to transform art and perception. They are also organic and cumulative in their genesis. I have stressed the tangible art activities which constitute the ground for their growth. The conscious and semi-literary form which the river theme took with me was, as I indicated, an emergence in the middle and not the early period of that theme. Had it not taken a written, commemorative form, it would be inaccessible now, for there are no transcribed interviews and the like to draw upon.

I do not think I am unique in this regard, except that the theme and form of the complex is peculiarly mine. I sense such funded meanings and superordinate concepts about making art in all of the artists I have studied, but I have lacked the extensive time span which would yield the larger views.

It is instructive that during the middle time period, when the fragments were written, I moved more toward extended paintings of the river theme, as time permitted, than toward drawings. The layers of meaning were more easily captured in a more complex medium. I also remember discovering through actual light and shade falling on top of represented light and shade on one of my paintings—a chance occurrence, but one for which I was "prepared"—a means whereby I could explore and symbolize the overlay of past and present I felt so poignantly with the river theme—lights within lights, and shadows within shadows.

The artistic serial encourages, in my view, the development of complex cognitive constructs about making art, and these can easily take the form of active world views which guide one at many levels of perception and performance. I believe I see the same phenomenon operating in my own pottery and in other potters I know. Because operations have their technical as well as symbolic component, pottery offers a still clearer example of how the seemingly purely technical decisions are guided by a complex conceptual system of values and meanings.

The reader may have discerned in the drawings and fragments of my own given above the origins of my emphasis on idiosyncratic meaning, personal causation, and the artistic serial which leads to the myth of self-identity and eventually to that more coherent system of concepts about making art which I have called the idiosyncratic artistic myth. The genesis of these ideas must be in such past events from my own history, although I was not conscious of them before in any theoretical sense. I realize that in sharing such material of an autobiographical nature I render myself vulnerable, but I persist in the belief that I am not that different from others, so that comparable superordinate concepts will be found in them, though always within their own individual textures of form and content.

Contemporary Life Styles and the Search
for a New Aesthetic

Trying to put together a book on alternative modes of inquiry into the making of art makes me both realize and admit that I am a child of an earlier generation. The seventeen-year-old son of a friend of mine has read through Heidegger's *Being and Time* twice already. Young undergraduate and graduate students are constantly trying to educate me concerning new life styles and newer art-life connections. It is more than a matter of the rapid succession of innovative art styles which followed rapidly upon Abstract Expressionism—the Pop, Op, Minimal,

Funk, Anti-Art, Intermedia Art, Environmental Art, Life Celebrations and Experiential Transcendence-Art, and the like.

Certainly, too, I have given evidence of movement toward existentialism and phenomenology, although the character of this influence is such that I can make no claim toward philosophical sophistication. I have followed my own empirical route. It is not a matter of abstract concepts but of dilemmas arising as I try to probe further into the making of art and am faced with problems of description and interpretation.

What I bring to these topics is some sense of history as the ground for my own transition. The seventeen-year-old reading Heidegger's difficult work cannot have the same sense of history and change. The young students who can easily see me as a traditional medium-centered artist hung up on object fetishism have come of age when activist politics, revolts, radicalism, the counter-culture, the Vietnam War, and the various liberation movements are pressing social realities. When I was at a comparable age, we were drifting into involvement in World War II. Certainly, to state the obvious, the texture of art and life has changed.

I offer these reflections, because I am self-conscious about how I have presented the idea of superordinate concepts concerning art which have directive and symbolic power in an artist's creations. Those I have studied lately have not been trained in the arts. They have, nonetheless, acted very much as artists. They are participants in the social-cultural milieu I have mentioned above, but I would have to admit that they are not at the leading edge of consciousness concerning the arts. From a contextual, research point of view, this does not matter. I am inclined to believe that individual artistic myths and the emergence of self-identity in art is a process of slow accretion and growth of consciousness, much as I have presented it in the case of Larry in chapter 4. But I am aware that the very concept of self, as related to art, has connotations today that my own youth lacked. It is as though the young have grasped at an identity beyond the familiar "identity crisis," and see this differently from our earlier emphasis on "commitment" and "works." Deliberate or accepted diffusion and confusion of identity and courting of intensive, direct "experiencing," have produced what the psychologist Robert Jay Lifton calls "Protean man"—an allusion to the Greek god who could change his shape and form with ease.[3] Lifton claims this style is not a pathological one, but an adaptive or even innovative one peculiar to the present. He also says, as in the mythological source, that Protean man finds it painful or difficult to commit himself to any form, especially one most his own, and that he is in constant danger of falling into the pitfall of "romantic totalism," which he describes as

> . . . a post-Cartesian absolutism, . . . a new quest for old feelings. Its controlling image, at whatever level of consciousness, is that of *replacing history with experience*.[4]

Earlier I found reason to object to Yeats' concept of the mask. The notion that there is no self to be expressed, but rather that the self is ever constructed in the doing relates Yeats' mask to the style of Protean man. With Yeats, and in me, the sense of historical continuity, however, remains important. Perhaps we should not seek the historical sense in the young. What we are witnessing is the plain fact that viable life styles are more clearly the creation of the young than when I came of age.

Why I digress in this fashion is to indicate that the kinds of superordinate concepts about making art can differ markedly from the examples I have given. It is the presence of these, not their similarity, for which I argue. I believe that many young artists will fight the kind of "historical self-determinism" to which I partially succumbed. We already saw Larry fighting the idea that he was trapped in a single line of development. In reviewing his works he said, "Each one is a different exploration. They don't culminate in anything." We have also seen the desire to make the drawing process vital and take precedence over the quality of a work or the problem of skill. Not that these are issues which need fall on one side or the other, but in the press the intensity of experience now comes first.

Maybe all that has changed is the pace and discipline of individual development. Those more in the Protean style want life and meaning *now* and on their own terms. There is not the slow discipline nurtured by a viable tradition with its solid sense of history and its subtle extension. If this is so, then the spirit is similar with untrained, naive artists and sophisticated more self-consciously innovative ones. I only mean to point out that the denial of historical continuity and the play with change of self are also ready raw materials for the development of artistic idiosyncratic myths.

6 Presentational, Historical, and Interpretive Modes in Complex Art-Making Situations

Difficulty of the Task of This Chapter

Where more than one artist is involved in making art in a given setting, as with individuals, we can outline varying expressive-presentational, historical and interpretive, particular theoretical and grounded abstract, and formative hermeneutic modes. We can also undertake existential-phenomenological reconstructions. As with the single artist, too, this chapter will stress the importance of sharing the co-acting artists' streams of consciousness and of special participant observer methods encouraging sharing and nuturance of the artistic dialogue. Whereas in the individually focused formative hermeneutic mode the effort was to synthesize the individual with the collective psyche, however, in this instance it is more like synthesizing the group, or nascent community, with the mythogenetic collective psyche and the collaborating individual psyches.

I find it difficult to describe modes appropriate to this chapter. A purely logical extension of all the modes discussed for inquiry into the individual artist's making of art is, on the surface, easily possible with co-acting artists. But as soon as I approach this simple logical extension, I hesitate. The social, political, institutional, and communal complexities that arise overwhelm me and make me very conscious of my limitations. I have tried to make this book more than an academic survey of methods, because I feel the modes I present are genuine alternatives close to my own experience. How cognitively and epistemologically adequate they are must await evaluation in the next chapter and in the mind of the reader. They are real to me. Now, however, I find I lack the ready material and the cumulative foundation in feeling required to undergird my descriptions and exemplifications of modes for the complex group situation.

The Crowd, The Machine, The Community and Art

People come together for many, many reasons. The very idea of culture rests on shared and sharable symbols, myths, and rituals, not to mention the countless facilitative roles and dependencies which are an accepted and necessary part of our complex civilization. We may be born and we may die alone and naked, but in between even the hermit lives in and is formed through an interpersonal world and its structures. The Protean self to which I alluded in the last chapter surely gains some of its changeable and changing style from the speed and variety of our encounters with others and from the sheer quantity of symbolic material impinging upon us moment by moment. The Psalmist asked whither he might go to flee the Lord. We could say the same about man, about information. We could say it even of our consciousness, wherein we move as in a steady stream of images, memories, feelings, intentions and meanings. We can flee neither ourselves nor man. The self is itself comprised of others. It is the insubstantial continuity of sameness through differences. Put otherwise, the self is the same, as Levinas puts it, unless it moves to the other, to otherness.[1] Sameness is not static: it is withdrawal, atrophy, death. We desire meaningful otherness.

We also know, and the young have vigorously attacked, meaningless and debilitating encounters with others. In these we do not move out to meet, from desire and not just need, the infinite enhancement we expect from free human encounter. Rather, we are thrown together like chance, unfeeling objects, or we are "totalized," utilized, processed by monstrous paper-based machines whose laws and conditions submerge all of our desire.

It has always happened, and always will, that the crowd, and the machines-of-people, are transcended. The weak "we" becomes the living community. Truly, even empty forms and institutions are often infinitesimally transcended. There is slippage at all the joints and human interaction spills over the roles and rules, usually gently, sometimes with force.

The essential living relationship with otherness, says Buber, exists over against things, people, and the mystery of life, moving toward art, love, and religion.[2] These are the "primary words" of existence. While art is one of these primary words, Buber sees it more as a movement of expression from the self forward or outward. By itself, art keeps the creator lonely and cut off from what can only come from the interhuman—mutuality and sharing. This is the sphere of love, of dialogue, of community.

In my own work in the drawing lab, as I have previously indicated, it has been necessary to begin with the assumption and belief that a genuine artistic dialogue is taking place or is always about to take place. Thus the existential and transcendental ingredients are there actually or potentially from the start. A reflexivity toward my own efforts at inquiry into the making of art has brought forth the working ethic that whatever I do in my studies should enhance the artist's freedom—his artistic casuality, idiosyncratic meaning, and intentional symbolization. Otherwise I "totalize" him, making him a part of some *a priori* system consciously applied. But, of course, even if I fight this tendency I come "structured" to my work. Only by moving out and toward the artist as to a genuine human encounter can I transcend the limits set by more narrowly conceived epistemological aims. The events that become the raw material for later attention can only be appreciated reflectively or interpreted in any manner as I move away from them in time and in level of abstraction. There, for purposes of extensionalization and proliferation of views, I can bear the arbitrariness of chosen perspectives.

Art and love, then, are commingled. The artist's producing consciousness is active and proactive, not reactive, but, in truth, imaginative and free in even the retroactive exploration of its own history. I try to relate fully to the artist in the present, testifying to the fact that his past and his future making of art are free.

I would argue that this is a miniature community with the artist's production of art its core and goal. My non-instructional and counter-interventionist role keeps the artist free. My effort to appreciate and understand him nurtures him and encourages him to share. Sharing is mutually productive: it brings him to a non-threatening extension of consciousness and me to knowledge of how he makes his art as viewed from this center of action.

Basis for the Group Inquiry

The contextualist view, as indicated in chapter 4, allows us to conceptualize the spread of events from the immediate present into the series (the drawing series), into a continuous "individual texture" which in turn can be situated within a still larger context. Thus we can move from a more private to a more public context without too much difficulty, so that what seems like a protected and bounded world breaks out into a larger one. By extension, then, what seems a miniature community connects with larger and fuller ones.

I have been interested in how inputs concerned with art from the larger culture come to the artist and are changed and assimilated by him. Unless these inputs are strong and discriminable they are unacknowledged in the bounded context of the drawing lab. Currently, we are studying three artists in the drawing lab in such a way that they will be protected in their privacy and uninterrupted and separate while they draw. After they become used to the drawing lab and to the feedback inquiry based on their previous week's drawing processes, we intend to have a group inquiry in which the recalled and explored inquiry sessions are shared among the three participants. By extending the individual's to the group's history we hope to be able to follow the interwoven strands of influences. This enlarged context symbolizes an explicit passage from the private to the communal art-making context. The role of the special participant observer remains the same, except now the possibility of interaction among the three artists disperses the human function of sharing and caring. To the degree that this happens, the special participant observer can shift attention to the art-makers in community, momentarily opening to his gaze the dynamics of relationships which are rendered more opaque when he is himself a full participant in a one-to-one dialogue with a single producing artist. Thus enters a rhythm of immersion and detachment hard to experience with a single artist. The ethic of relationship, however, still requires, from my view, that the presence of the special participant observer enhance that existential and potential community of working artists of which he is a part.

I can conceive that the researcher's role will now absorb new functions. On a second level of reflection he will doubtlessly be exploring the group's review of the individual but shared inquiries. The feelings, evaluations, and projections resulting raise the inquiry to new levels of complexity and consciousness. These will feed into subsequent drawings, thence into the individual inquiries, thence into the shared interaction on the individual inquiries, and so on. Each context is honored as a unique historical problem, and, as earlier suggested, we probe a peculiarly open, pluralistically-conceived history, wherein we try to extensionalize and open up the uniqueness and infinity of expressive situations. Its proper and even ecstatic end may well be the appreciation of the complexity, openness, and situationally specific structure of expressive acts, and how these participate in both man's finiteness and freedom.

The difficulty with inquiry into the group art setting is that the purpose of research becomes politicized very easily. Groups come into existence as "political communities." There are reasons for the making and remaking of groups. We cooperate according to certain norms. Access to the group, for purposes of inquiry, is under the scrutiny of the group's power structure, or else the one inquiring comes "representing" another group whose norms have explicit connections with the group under study. As earlier indicated, Gouldner in his discussion of a reflexive sociology dispels the illusion that the researcher is neutral.[3] He is for or against, he enhances or he detracts.

In education we obviously deal in value structures whenever we enter into "evaluative research" of the curriculum or of any of its components. The shift from "summative" to "formative" evaluation seems to put the power back into the hands of the actors. It is a cybernetic, process focus. "Accountability" takes the power away and gives it to a power group encircling the group under study. As for the artist, he

> specializes in the manipulation of the symbolic structure. He tends generally to communicate by reaffirming the norms of the co-operative structure. (And when discrediting one of the norms, he usually does so by affirming another of the norms; he pits one of his society's values against another of its values, so that even in an attitude of "rejection," he is not wholly "outside" the values of his society.)[4]

But what are the norms of the cooperative structure in the case of a group of artists working together and how does the artist manipulate these? And what is the position of the researcher with regard to these norms and their manipulation? These are the hard questions.

A graduate advisee of mine is acting as a participant observer in public school art classes. Specifically, he is attempting a contextualist description and analysis of settings where a student teacher is involved. His focus is the student teacher in the teaching-learning context of the classroom. To enter into such studies, he must pass through many points of review and clearance in the power structure. Ostensibly he wants to reconstruct change, development, regression, whatever, in the art student teacher. But explict and incidental curricula are in operation, the ends of which are much more important than the development of the student teacher. The entrance of the participant observer raises the question of his influence for good or ill and the concern about what the knowledge he seeks is for. No one sees it as neutral, apparently. The principal, the teacher supervising, the student teacher, and others would like some feedback. They would like to get some use from the permitted study.

My advisee can disclaim any teaching or influencing function, but his interest in the setting and the feedback he provides (and cannot help providing to some degree) become nurturant or supportive of values in the co-operative structure. The more he interacts to gain knowledge—as, for example, in meeting with the supervising teacher or the student teacher to see what was intended, how it worked from the other's view—the more he reflects information helpful in the observed person's self-direction and self-evaluation. Even when the observed person's self-perception is negative, when the participant observer accepts or acknowledges that feeling non-judgmentally, it comes to rest against norms of the group structure. The reflection has helped it to do so.

One is "in on the history," which perforce becomes "one is *in* the history." What might seem to be contaminating is not so if it is acknowledged that human affairs can only be conceived as movements around the norms of cooperative structures. No one is above or below these conditions. The vulnerability of the researcher and the necessity for reflexivity regarding his own consciousness and experience are the price of knowledge of the human, of man in context. (The story of the sociologists who went to study Billy Graham's revival meetings, where several of the researchers ended up at the altar, is more than just a joke. It becomes facetious only in carrying the vulnerability further than we would expect.)

Let me reiterate the two prime assumptions of this book: (1) In studying expressive situations, we do not deal with aesthetic behavior units, because aesthetic experience is above all a psychic reality. Our concern is with the psychic reality of the aesthetic experience within the artist's stream of consciousness in the unique expressive situation. (2) As researchers we must act as special participant observers if we are to gain access to the internal events and the guidance system at work in the unique expressive situation. A serial and contextual perspective are most appropriate procedurally to these assumptions, as is some means of reflected history wherein indirect access to the artist's stream of consciousness is both sharable with the participant observer and useful to the artist.

Such assumptions have led me to the gradual formation of a co-operative structure in which the values of making art and sharing are central. Under the aegis of research, the established group (or potential community) lies somewhat protected from the curriculum and rules of the sheltering institution. The manipulation of the symbolic structure is in the artist's hands, where it belongs, and where he can reaffirm or discredit the norms of the co-operative group in consonance with his own meanings and sense of causation. Now, when I add other artists, so that we have a group of artists, the emergent cooperative structure and its norms become a descriptive, historical problem. How do the artists get along with each other? What is the nature of their life together? What strands lead into and out from the group? What conceptions about making art and prizing art are operative? What is the quality of the artists' lives together like, as opposed to the setting where the single artist is the core, where the peculiarities and changes of his own meanings and methods are foremost?

The descriptive and analytical problem, seen from the contextualist view, is that of confronting unique historical events. This is far from simple, nay, it is even impossible, as any reflective writing on the problem of history reveals. But our problem is confounded, for we deal with events we have termed psychic, only indirectly accessible, and that only under special conditions. But there are methods, there are categories, as our flirtation with contextualism has demonstrated. If ours is a special kind of history, this is only because the unique events of concern are experiential ones which include the artist and include us too. They include us as facilitating, or failing to, and the artist as creating and sharing, or failing too. From there on, our modes try to present, reconstruct, appreciate, or analyze as much as we can, or, as Pepper puts it, until we tire, for there is literally no end of the process. In giving up the *a priori* of science, which allows for clarity and control of form, we have inherited the existential and experiential complexity and dispersion of shared history. We claim as positive the reflexiveness of the researcher's role and his effort, in time, to remove himself by degrees from nearly complete immersion in the events to levels of abstraction where his very biases become tools of analysis.

Perhaps the subtleties of inquiry into the making of art when the latter is conceived as in the artist's hands can be illustrated by a comparison with a complex setting where the focus is on acts and meanings established by expectancy before we enter as participant observers. Louis M. Smith has pioneered in studies of what he calls the micro-ethnography of the classroom.[5] Trained as an educational researcher and a social scientist, he has expectations and goals for his research which I cannot entertain from a contextualist, historical viewpoint. He wishes, for example, to develop grounded theories of teaching which will lead to more abstract models, eventually toward a general theory of teaching which can be put to empirical test. Our view of the uniqueness of events does not encourage this hope. Any generalizations risked come out of the perspective of the type concept or the container concept modes presented earlier (chap. 4).

But at the earlier stages of inquiry, Smith operates much as I believe I try to. He describes a given context from his position as an observer. In the example I shall give, he is part of an evaluation team for an aesthetic education project which has produced "packages" for use in the elementary schools. The packages have explicit content, procedures, objectives, and the like. They thus represent relatively known inputs into given class settings. Part of Smith's role is to describe utilization and facilitation from one setting to another, toward the end of package improvement, in-service training and supervison of teachers, summative evaluation of packages and programs, and the like. Below is a "vignette" from Smith's April 3, 1972, Memo.

VIGNETTE

This morning at 10:25 a.m. I observed my first class using the meter package. For a musical illiterate, it proved to be a fascinating experience. The 28 children (second and third graders in an open environment) were grouped in two semi-circles with center stage shared by Chart #4, the phonograph, and two children, each with what looked like a homemade drum head. The teacher, who seemed comfortable with the materials, explained "accents" as "louder" or "stronger" beats and indicated that the children should make a fist for the hard beats and use an open hand for the soft taps. Her directions blended with explanations as she indicated "bar lines," "measures," and "duple" and "triple" meter. The two children had little trouble reading the music and performing as musicians. This activity was rotated through several pairs of children, each of whom selected his successor. Spliced into the activity was a total group performance. The children clapped the several lines of music in duple and triple meter with appropriate accents. Throughout, participation and involvement were high. The facial expressions were of pleasure. The teacher made almost no comments of a disciplinary sort. (In a later part of the lesson, considerable contrast occurred.)

The teacher flowed in and out of the lesson in what might be called "goal facilitation interventions," that is, when problems occurred which hindered accomplishment she found a way to move in, momentarily help, and move out. The best example occurred with a child or two who couldn't use the drum head. As though she were teaching a psychomotor skill, she reached around the child, held the drum and the child's hand, and started the appropriate duple or triple meter. When the child caught on, she carried on alone. Later illustrations of the same sort occurred in the total group clapping. For instance, the teacher would clap in exaggerated fashion, particularly with each new line and new beat. In the middle section of activities she went from table to table where the children were having difficulty. As she said "Listen!" she would tap on the table with exaggerated and obvious motions, the beats and accents. As the children understood, even momentarily, she would move on.

The middle part of the day's activity consisted of listening to Activity 7 and recording on Response Sheet 3. Once the response sheets had been passed out, the teacher began the record. The children had difficulty following the directions, hearing the meter, and getting responses recorded on the sheets. The teacher (and the principal who was visiting) moved about helping the children, as indicated earlier. The kids seemed puzzled, their faces and actions were not of clarity, they looked at each other and each other's papers, they raised their hands for the teacher. Progressively, as they worked through the three illustrations, more playing with pencils, reading library books, and chattering occurred. Concurrently, through this twenty minutes, more teacher comments, "shushes" and "sit right in your seat" directions appeared.

The final fifteen minutes took the form of a total class review, "go over the materials so you understand," of the record and identification of the meter and noting of accents. This turned out to be a "mild disaster." The teacher drew the meter charts on the black board. She tried to stay ahead by alternating between two boards, one on the south wall and one on the west wall. She had a pupil go to the board and indicate meter and accent for each. They had some problems. In spite of several mild reprimands, two girls persisted in playing with the drum heads; they alternated in reading Chart 4 and trying to keep time with the music on the record. The teacher's comments, "Listen carefully boys and girls. Most of you aren't listening," seemed both accurate and necessary. She did the last part "once again" over the growing distraction and resistance of the children for she was concerned that they understand. Her last comment was "I think we'll have to do it over again. Some of you haven't got it yet." At 11:13 they started to set up for an ETV science lesson about the "moon."[6]

In this vignette we have a good example of description of a complex setting, where the material collected refers to purposes outside the setting (the aesthetic education project), to definite materials and procedures (the aesthetic education package), and to how these fare in the hands of a teacher in in-service training. Smith's report deals with unique historic events, seen through his eye, as these bear on such purposes.

It is done well and economically. It reflects a more successful with a less successful occasion related to different parts of the package. Smith refers to implications and meanings of the vignette.[7] We will refer to three of the six points he makes:

(2) the first part seemed to reflect the recreator or performer role. More precisely the children, individually and collectively, read the chart, clapped or beat time on the drum, and "talked music." They were in the adient end of the involvement continuum—toward joy.

(3) parts #2 and #3 seemed more in the appreciator/listener/audience role. Affect moved toward the non-involved and avoidant end of the continuum. (An active/passive dimension may need to be built into the model.)

(4) the reasons, or causes, of the events is another set of issues, e.g., the lesson was too long, the music is too complicated, the teacher knows music, the open environment is congruent with performing but not appreciating, etc. These hypotheses involve a set of analyses for another occasion.

In reading Smith's implications we learn that he has come to his task not only with role purposes fairly clearly in mind (his function as evaluator for the aesthetic education project) and inputs clearly tagged (the aesthetic education package, the in-service training program), but also with a systematic three-dimensional model conceptualizing aesthetic education (the latter is discussed in earlier memos and contains: (1) six art forms, (2) five pupil roles, and (3) kind of affective involvement). Thus he can refer to pupil roles and kind of affective involvement, and relate these back to the package and the class context (which he does in implications 2 and 3 above). These references lead him to "causes" or "reasons" (implication 4 above) which are reflected back to the package, the teacher, the environment.

Here, in miniature, we see a highly skilled researcher at work. It might be said that he works out of a functional context (his evaluation role in the aesthetic education program), a theoretical context (his model of aesthetic education, his long-range interest in a general theory of teaching), and, of necessity, an historical context (the setting out of which the vignette arose). What, however, is Smith's purpose primarily? That, too, is complex, but perhaps I can clarify my own position toward "group" studies by comparison with his.

Counelis in a recent article has attempted a typology of generic research designs which attracted me because it makes useful distinctions I have not found in other typologies.[8] A major dimension of his typology deals with the researcher's time/space assumptions. He says there are two of these: the kairotic time/space manifold, which derives from a Greek word for time which "refers to the unique moments in a temporal process that emphasize the qualitative, the experiential, and the singular;" and the *chronotic,* also of Greek origin, which "refers to the quantitative, calculable, and repetitive elements in the temporal process."[9] The second dimension of Counelis' typology is akin to Plato's distinction between the one and the many, or the *unit* object and *the object class.* Below is the typology constructed of these two dimensions:

Scientist's Assumptions About Time and Space

		Kairotic Manifold	Chronotic Manifold
Objective Characteristic of Object Under Study	Unit Object	History	The Case
	Class Object	The Survey	The Experiment

A Typology of Generic Research Designs[10]

Counelis offers the following descriptions:

> History and biography are concerned with the one, the unique object/event with a particular time/space locus.
> Though surveys are built upon frequencies of the *unit,* it is with the *class* of the unique . . . that the survey is concerned primarily.
> Case study is alway a study of the singular, be it a person, an institution, a social group, or some other social system . . . The case is understood, usually, as a generalized microcosm; or better, the case is understood as a Hegelian concrete general.
> The epistemic rule in experimental design is to control all sources of variance and uniqueness explicitly.[11]

The above typology clarifies that the emphasis of this book is on the kairotic time/space manifold and the unit object. It is, in fact, history, with all of its problems. Whether I speak of a single artist or a group of artists, this is my perspective. It is obvious that I use the word "case" differently from Counelis. Only when I refer to the case under the "type concept" does it take on some of the connotation of a "Hegelian concrete general," and that only weakly.

Perhaps only "the general" can be "understood," and only "the unique" formed, enjoyed, appreciated (the qualitative, the experiential, and the singular), and that is why I have drifted toward history and toward contextualism as particularly appropriate for the study of the making of art.

Smith, on the other hand, is concerned with the Hegelian concrete general. Like Erik Erikson's use of cases for a dynamic theory of childhood growth, Smith is hopeful for a general theory of teaching. I am led toward situational analysis, toward a rummaging around among qualitative phenomena, toward an extensionalization of what, at bottom, is the unknowable quality of unique events. Smith, if I read him rightly, is led toward implications, reasons, explanations, and eventually laws and control (toward the experiment).

At the first level, there is not a great dissimilarity in method—we both try to begin with a "picture" of the reality. Nor is there purism. I tend toward weak "general theories" at times, and Smith is certainly patient and careful to a fault, going day after day, week after week, to the same classroom and taking careful field notes, transcribing impressions, having coffee each morning with the teacher he observed.[12] Both Smith and the modes of this book stay close to the unit object. The purposes of knowledge and where the knowledge leads differ. In my case, only the "container concept" (pooled cases) leads toward the class object. Perhaps, too, there is a tacit "theory of art education" behind much of my effort, but I doubt it and prefer to claim pluralism on that score, whereas in research I am content with an enlargement of wonder and appreciation.

At this point, let us discuss the various modes of inquiry which are applicable to the group setting and which can operate under the major assumptions of this book. As I have indicated, I will not try to present examples of these modes since they are not yet a part of my own experience.

Iconic Representations of the Group Setting

For readers in the visual arts it may be unnecessary to detail the possibilities of modes of mute evidence: still photography, motion picture, television, environmental sound tapes of high fidelity, and the like. In one sense these "speak for themselves," but certainly they do not analyze or interpret themselves. They are "the given," and come as close to the event, undistorted, it would seem, as we can get.

But do they really? The lens is not an eye and the microphone is not an ear. Further, these are activated, directed, positioned, edited, spliced, printed, and the like, by the human hand and mind, so that a built-in perspective is implied, with that distortion we try to avoid built in from the start. If one is technologically astute, the case is even more delicate, for then we will be sensitive to lenses, the grain of negative and paper, the frequency ranges of the microphone and amplifier, the lighting on the television set, and so on.

Still, phenomena so captured are close to the event, and we accept the fact that we come to all events through some selectivity, some position and perspective. We can multiply perspectives, too, as in using three T.V. cameras on the same scene, subsequently or simultaneously monitored into one event stream. In short, we could say nothing and come at a setting with *all* of the media technology we could amass. In the end we would merely have a different kind of beginning point to represent the phenomena which are the start, not the end, of our inquiry. Cameras are not reflexive, only the humans using them. And cameras do not know the problems of contamination or disengagement.

The point worth making here is that we have not begun to use media in terms of their potential, especially as means for iconic depiction of complex settings, such as we have in schools, field projects, group studios, and the like. Such recorded events as we might obtain could take care of some of the problem of communicating affective factors in a given situation. For the participant observer, there is little problem in reviving his bare field notes, even years later, because he was there, he lived it. For anyone not so involved, certainly iconic representations of the setting would flesh the notes out.

During the summers, for several years now, I have engaged an advanced ceramics class in communal pottery activities close to the primitive terms of the craft. We have dug our own clay, built our own kilns (away from the school), gathered our own wood, and carefully tended fires, sometimes for as long as sixty hours running. The sense of community and purpose arising out of shared labors, hardships, successes and failures is something that must be experienced for comprehension. I could labor in words to try to evoke the feel of one of these groups, but it would take masterful writing, more like literature than simple description, to do so.

If you, the reader, had participated, however, the feel in your hand of one of the cruddy pots which survived and the stimulus of a photograph or two (as in fig. 18) would suffice to evoke a rich reconstruction of the whole. You would get the feeling better as an outsider, however, were I to have you join me and several other participants with a collection of their cruddy pots, an evening of slides and motion picture sequences on some of the activities, and some parallel activities to fill in our present experience and connect it with the past (let's say we just came from digging some new clay).

All of this, you will surely say, is commonplace, is commonsense. It is also absurd. So it is. Inquiry begins there and moves toward critical refinement of the same phenomena.

First-person-singular and Multiple-consciousness Narrative of Group Settings

If, while such communal activities were occurring, participant observers had been with us, their field notes would augment and preserve much that is in our stills, slides, motion pictures, pots, and "evaluations" (really written "testimonials" of involvement). Further, such self-conscious historians would have one eye on the record, not just on immersion in experience. They would be "faithful" to their role. No matter how tired, they would complete the field note entry for the day, perhaps before or after their time on a wood-stoking crew. They might tape-record reactions (as one student did during our first kiln-opening at the hillside kiln), or interview various group members. They might gauge morale, peer pressures, factions, emergent leadership, ratio of "successful" pots to failures or to broken ones.

Figure 18. Communal pottery kiln building and firing

They would certainly collect and analyze such statements as these (excerpted from 1971 self-evaluations, each paragraph from a different student):

> This type of project produced a closer working relationship with all persons involved. During this relationship many attitudes other than art were brought out. People became friends rather than just classroom acquaintances. Through my contributions to the community project I received much personal satisfaction. I only hope I can impart these same feelings to my students in class.

> . . . .

> Last year's group was better able to organize itself than this summer. Your plan of attack which you outlined for the second firing seemed to work well. Your consideration for suggested guidelines would be most helpful for any future "community projects." All efforts to continue your "Summer Madness" should be furthered. Maybe fate will join together a more "fraternal" group. Last year there was a much greater respect by the group for the *communal* atmosphere of the course. This year I think the vastness of the engineering fete [sic] and structure superseded that longed-for true communal return to "pre-technology" methodology of firing ceramics.

> . . . .

> As for the matter of self-evaluation, including a letter grade, I find some of my suspected feelings concerning this term's class to be confirmed. I recall that last year you felt embarrassed to even mention grades. Your change in attitude reflects the difference between the two classes. I see that difference possibly being reflected in the number of people seeking three credits as opposed to those seeking a total immersion in the craft.

> . . . .

> This has been the most event-filled, fun-filled, growth-filled, beautiful-filled summer of my life.
> I wouldn't have missed the experience of stoking for anything in the world. Just to understand the gentleness of the kiln, and how the pieces of wood you threw in had to complement each other, how important the rhythm was, was exciting. But most important as I know all the kids felt was the feeling of being part of a group. We were not just students and you were not just a teacher. This is where education really begins. I only hope that someday I will be able to do what you did for all of us, to pass on a life-long memory to my students.

> . . . .

> I wasn't prepared for what really happened but fortunately no preparation was necessary. It is difficult to explain what really did happen—it was more an evolution than a happening. The core element to this evolution was people—people doing something together in a very natural way. People standing in sloppy sticky goo and being excited by its change in color and purity. Jobs being done by people who weren't asked to do them—whose only payments were blisters, sunburn, insect bites, sore muscles and a feeling of satisfaction.
> The wonder is that though this effort led to failure this group of people failed with more enthusiasm than others do in succeeding. Failure did not disorganize this group but instead tended to unite them even more.
> The above is a rather superficial report of what a group of people did and how they outwardly reacted (or seemed to react to me). There was, however, some mysterious element in the clay, bricks, wood, fire and air that motivated these people and it is beyond me to explain. As a member of the group, you understand what I mean but others (outsiders) might never understand.

I could go on with such statements (perhaps I am trying to increase my motivation and energy level for more "summer madness"), but that would be to lose my path. (In passing, notice what my sampling would be like had I left out the second and third excerpt.) As I was saying, participant observers, had they been present, would have been interested in such things. All meaningful scraps, artifacts, iconic modes of evidence, interviews, field notes, individual diaries, and the like would be blocks for reconstructing the phenomenon referred to as "Old Man Biddle's Summer Madness."

Out of the mass of collected material, participant observers could reasonably fashion a convincing documentary, a narrative of multiple-consciousness type. Inserted into this would be, doubtlessly, innumerable first-person-singular statements (one source of which, I almost forgot, would be my own as teacher). But the multiple-consciousness format would allow for descriptions which can shift perspective. At one point "the class" can be described in its dispersed or integrated activities. "Outsiders" views could come in. Then a direct statement of a participant might appear, as in a work of fiction.

The aim of all of this would be presentational, in either the expressive or more neutrally descriptive sense (a feeling of sympathy, empathy, but with some distance). I am insisting on a grasp of complexity and change close to the chain of lived unique events in their proper context. It should be, I am saying, an effort at historical reconstruction.

Historical Modes in the Group Setting

Contextual analysis would have us honor unique events in all their vividness. We would begin, that is, with some grasp of that pervasive quality which stains all situations we experience. Hence the prior discussion of naturalistic reconstruction of phenomena in all their experienced fullness. The quality of the events in context is intuitively grasped by the experiencing consciousness, but that intuition is not directly communicable. As in the categories under Pepper's discussion of contextualism,[13] it is necessary to explore and analyze the textures within the contexts under scrutiny; and to do so, the researcher turns toward the many "strands" of which a texture is comprised, and to the various references of strands which permit analysis of the patterns and relationships occurring among strands. (The reader is referred to Pepper's book, *World Hypotheses*, for the full presentation of contextualism, its categories, and its truth theory.)

As my discussion earlier in this chapter on "basis for the group inquiry" indicates, one of the "foreshadowed problems" to which I am inclined is that of inquiry into the kinds of self-directing concepts about making art which are held, expanded, transformed, or rejected at some point by any given artist. In the group setting, I am much interested in the way such regulative conceptualizations find support or denial in existing and emergent norms of the cooperating group. I find it useful, perhaps because of my own conceptualizations about art education and about making art, to start with analysis of the qualitative nature of concepts about making art as these are found in the life context of the individuals within the group. By this I mean that I like to see such concepts first in action in a drawing series of an individual artist, largely apart from a group context. Once, then, these strands have been identified, I can follow them into and, possibly, out of the group situation. My reasoning here is that the individual artist, for all the potent cultural and social forces shaping him, nurtures, almost as an artistic myth, his idiosyncratic approach. He is not just a cubist or an abstract expressionist. He is Gris or Braque; he is deKooning or Guston. Even with the Protean life style alluded to, a dynamic, changing personality is perforce unique in each of its incarnations. This need not be a conscious aim. It is an inevitable part of the historical or contextual view that each individual, just as each event, is radically unique and different.

This preference for how to begin is a procedural one. It also says the obvious: the basic unit in art is the artist. He moves into and out of groups and institutions, but unless he stops producing, the artistic serial continues. Even in my earlier experiments related to drawing strategies,[14] it was important to sense the pre-treatment base and the post-treatment status of the participants. Further, as I tried to suggest in chapter 5, artists are prone to develop quite abstract superordinate concepts about the making of art, and these not only can persist for years or for a lifetime, but they also can keep lesser concepts in some hierarchical order. Thus, even when, say, new techniques or new symbols are picked up in a group setting, these are likely to change subtly their meaning upon assimilation into the acquiring artist's series. I have watched this process indirectly through the kinds of influences participants in our drawing lab picked up as they took formal art studios. In the few cases I have been able to follow up in this way, the newly acquired influences had a much better fit to the pre-existing base in the artist's series than to what the instructor of the class felt central in his teaching. What was central to the artist was incidental to the teacher, and vice versa. Nevertheless, the influence ostensibly came from the class setting.

The artistic self echoes the old French saying—the more it changes, the more it remains the same. The seemingly stereotyped, repetitive artist is very hard to see as a personality, as an individual. We must come closer to him and overcome our natural distaste for what is static and unchanging. Then we see, setting aside our own taste, that there are subtleties of emphasis, arrangement, content and technique (unless the case is near pathological, in which instance it is no less interesting to relate to), which are the signs of life, of an open system, no matter how restrictive its boundaries.

Such sensitivity to change on the part of a special participant observer is itself a function of a historical perspective. Perception, it is said, involves implicit judgment—a scanning of information for confirmation or disconfirmation. This is especially so in interpersonal knowing where we project our expectancies of another's behavior (and where the other person often obligingly conforms to our general hypotheses about him, so that in normal affairs the world can run habitually and smoothly). If we are attentive, we are always learning new things, because our general hypotheses cannot perfectly match the here and now. And if we go further and try to fully relate to the other, as an I to a thou, in the face-to-face, not only do we gain new information, we feel ourselves changed. When we find nothing new in the other, we have thickened the bars for our own imprisonment in the sameness of a static world.

In our present context, where we are concerned with the artistic serial in all its concreteness, our perception cannot function sensitively until we have built up a fund of unique events to draw upon. I saw this dramatically just recently when I and other participant observers tried to conduct a feedback inquiry with three artists, together for the first time as a group sharing each others' recollected drawings under the stimulus of time-lapse process shots. The questions we asked of the artists did not, as I feared, disturb them. They made very little contact with them at all. Why? Because we, as observers, were in our first group setting and did not have the wisdom and patience to just listen and look, or, at the very least, take our cues from the statements and the perceptions of the artists themselves. Instead, we imported questions from outside the context. They were, you might say, fantasies and fictions about the group setting. But, then, maybe the best correction was to project these wild expectancies and learn that they made no contact with the perception of the artists we were studying.

I have had a kind of rule for myself in the drawing lab which has arisen naturally over the last five years: I refuse to think much about an artist I am observing on the basis of one session in the lab. There is too little that is concrete and experiential about my relationship with him for me to internalize him and his artistic serial. With session two, and especially by session three, he has a history and a path. By session three he has done his first drawings, reflected on the history of these in the inquiry, done his second set of drawings, and reflected on these; so that the reflection on the impact of the earlier reflection on his drawings is already there in simplest form. Then I find it possible for me to conceive of the artist as an autonomous agent caught in the unpredictable and irreversible stream of concrete events but nonetheless constructing meanings fore and aft as he moves.

This seemingly simple setting is in reality so *complex* that I find myself, again without plan, taking a middle ground as to the amount of information I can handle as a human recording instrument. This middle ground is symbolized in a direct way by where I position myself in the drawing lab. When the inquiry session takes place, I sit lower than the artist and slightly to the side, between him and the wall upon which we project the time-lapse shots of his last drawings. I am between him and his history, inferior in position, but able to relate to him face to face while he talks or while I question him. (We have found it quite essential to be able to relate face to face with the artist when we question or stimulate his recall. Only in this way can we respond sensitively to his perceptions and feelings.) Once the inquiry is over, I remove myself to a desk outside the artist's studio, out of sight, where I make my longhand summary of the inquiry (allowing myself to make inferences, raise questions, echo back and project forward, as well as attempting to describe what was said and disclosed). One of my assistants will then monitor the camera, where, through a window, he can closely observe (off the front-surface mirror) the drawing as it actually evolves (but see little else, apart from the hand that is drawing). From this vantage point information is obtainable again through the human instrument other than what comes through the feedback inquiry. This assistant takes notes as well as controlling the camera. My other assistant sits just outside the artist's work area, to his rear. Here he is accessible if the artist needs anything. But he can also observe the artist's general condition if he wishes to—his posture, concentration, boredom, and the like.

Coming to the feedback inquiry without information of the drawings to be reviewed, I find myself attentive to the time-lapse records and to the artist's recall and feelings in a direct way. Whatever information my assistants have gathered augments and extends the basic material, which to me is the shared reconstruction of the artist's stream of consciousness as he made his drawings. No information beyond this is irrelevant, but I position myself on this middle ground. From this base I can add on or take away.

Recall close to the making but without the process records is conceivable, but it cannot be as good as the more iconic focus on the same events shared from two different first-person positions. True, if I am allowed to interpolate my questions between each session or completed work of an artist, some reconstruction is possible even though I and my assistants were not there when the work was done; but my grasp of those events seems more problematic, paler. I am trying this method now with an artist, because certainly I cannot have every artist I wish to study work in a laboratory setting, nor will every artist want to submit to the gathering of in-process records of his works. If I studied a poet, a composer, or an inventor who worked his creations out in his head, I would have no records beyond the finished work, his recall and whatever other observations were possible. In this regard, drawing is an ideal artistic activity for psychological study, for while the agency of the artist is here, too, largely covert, the events of construction leave their traces in the world where we can observe and record them.

But my effort in this section is to talk about historical modes in the group setting. I must accept the necessity to synthesize the individual and the community. Further, though I speak of presentational and more expressive modes in several parts of this book, yet I acknowledge that history and not art is the model of knowledge I must hold to. And when I attempt to speak of pooled cases and find myself repelled by such "container categories" and *a priori* abstractions (even when they are claimed to be "inductive"), then I likewise acknowledge that my model is history and not science. Contextualism, then, is the most comfortable world view

I can find. But I am not yet in the critique section of this book, so rather than reveal the difficulty, even impossibility, of my task, I would do better to continue my search for models and examples.

I have found my readiest model in anthropologists, who must confront statistical facts, their own experiences and perceptions, and on the basis thereof present the life of a village, or a culture. In his book, *Argonauts of the Western Pacific*, Malinowski has helpfully put together a chapter entitled "The Subject, Method and Scope of This Inquiry."[15] I believe the reader will find Malinowski's reflections in this chapter applicable to our present concerns.

First, Malinowski points out that we come to our work prepared. By training, through our studies, through theory, we bring problems with us to the field. These we must constantly revise, and willingly, as our experience and evidence dictate. "Preconceived ideas are pernicious in any scientific work, but foreshadowed problems are the main endowment of a scientific thinker. . . ."[16]

Secondly, the worker in the field must have his eye on the totality of the phenomena confronting him. Though coming with "foreshadowed problems" and more attentive to one aspect of the culture than another, he must not artifcially restrict his attention. He must pay attention to the commonplace as well as the dramatic. Further, what I would call a law of contextualism applies: "The consistency, the law and order which obtain within each aspect make also for joining them into one coherent whole."[17]

The worker in the field must depict and give the anatomy of regularities and forms which are operative around him but not available in abstract form. He must himself collect concrete evidence and then draw general inferences. The things he is trying to infer, however,

> . . . though crystallized and set, are nowhere formulated. There is no written or explicitly expressed code of laws, and their whole tribal tradition, the whole structure of their society, are embodied in the most elusive of all materials: the human being. But not even in human mind or memory are these laws to be found definitely formulated.[18]

Related to this problem is the advice not to approach a native with questions about abstract, general rules. Much better is a real occurrence in the life of the native which becomes the stimulus for opinions and information concerning the abstract concept the field worker is probing. By such means, over a number of occasions, information on a certain issue is rounded out. It then turns out that such material is usually part of still some bigger, more abstract concept. Malinowski suggests that the field worker project in writing short preliminary sketches of what he thinks he knows on a certain subject. Only thereby does he become aware of the gaps and deficiencies in the evidence he has thus far obtained.[19] Since there is no end to history, to contextualism, there will always be gaps, but by such checking devices glaring oversights can be corrected before it is too late.

There are, says Malinowski, three avenues or levels through which the goal of ethnographic field-work must be approached. These, roughly, correspond to skeleton, flesh and blood, and spirit:

> 1. *The organization of the tribe, and the anatomy of its culture* must be recorded in firm, clear outline. The method of *concrete, statistical documentation* is the means through which such outline has to be given.
> 2. Within this frame, the *imponderabilia of actual life*, and the *type of behavior* have to be filled in. They have to be collected through minute, detailed observations, in the form of some sort of ethnographic diary, made possible by close contact with native life.
> 3. A collection of ethnographic statements, characteristic narrative, typical utterances, items of folk-lore and magical formulae has to be given as a *corpus inscriptionum*, as documents of native mentality.[20]

Similar avenues to our goal exist: that of statistical, concrete documentation; the diary grasping for the "imponderabilia of actual life" through our patient immersion in intimate experience with others; and the personal documents and transcriptions of conceptions and values which others hold toward the making of art in group and individual settings.

Likewise, our concerns seem to follow the line of Malinowski's earlier methodological admonitions. We, too, come with "foreshadowed problems" which guide us, but in an open fashion always correctable through experience and evidence. In patience we must take in the trivial as well as the dramatic leaps, and be content if nothing at all seems to be occurring. We cannot restrict our attention, even though guided by special interests, for the whole and the part are presupposed each by the other. We must find what laws, regularities or patterns there may be by experiencing them in *operation,* for they have no *a priori* formulation. They exist in the lives of the persons we study, but not in a conscious sense, so that we cannot question them outright about them. We, too, do better to proceed from concrete occurrences in the lives and works of the artists, and to a method preserving their perceptual viewpoint.

The ethnographic methods of Malinowski, then, provide comfort for our own microethnographic ventures into individual and group settings where art is being made. The artistic ideal of "pure imagination" has its being in an infinity of diverse, concrete, far from perfect unique situations, and the contextual reconstruction and analysis of these is a historical problem. The individual and the community artistic serials constitute historical forms possessing coherence and boundaries sufficient to attract us to the task of description and interpretation.

I, personally, am just moving into the group artistic serial, so I cannot, and will not, attempt to speak with any authority concerning it. I do know that I am forced to try to synthesize the impossible but real split between the individual and the community in coming to this new study. Previously, I revealed my preference for following individual artist's serials into and out of the group art setting. I do so because art, of all areas of human experience and despite the prevalence of styles and traditions, seems at bottom a matter of individual agency, intention and meaning. The impossible ideal of pure imagination in conflict with an all too real, concrete situation, loses its meaning altogether when removed from the perceiving-acting-feeling of a given person, place and time.

Formative Hermeneutic Modes in the Group Setting

In similar fashion, I cannot speak with any confidence of this mode of inquiry and interaction when I come to the group setting. Still, as a category of method, it fascinates me, for it makes explicit the influence of the knower upon his supposed object. Nay, it goes further, it takes responsibility, ethically, for this influence.

I must confess that in the individual artistic serial I have likewise hesitated to move toward the formative hermeneutic mode. My brand of reflection and reflexivity have made my own knowing a central problem. I have had little or no desire to consciously direct or help the other, in my role of knowing. His action, I hoped, would seem to him a function of his own condition and path. I would follow from behind, in all my humanity, but not take the lead. How indeed could anyone take the lead for another's imagination? Yet, having said this, I acknowledge readily the interactive, synergetic impact of one human being upon another. Already as I have observed artists beginning to share their worlds with each other, the influences are just there, in the shared world, to be taken up, assimilated and transformed, or ignored, refused or strongly moved away from. They are, then, part of the situation of individual and group serials. I have revealed my tentative belief that influences will seem incidental to their source but central to their point of assimilation. That is, if X comes from artist A and is assimilated (in some recognizable though changed form) by artist B, X will seem central to the perceptual world of B but incidental to the world of A.

In the case of group tasks and the spiritual sense of true community, something other than the making of art is involved. In the performing arts and in the so-called mass media, something like the "group artistic serial" exists, but that term is hard for me to use with much meaning. I have not studied it with the intent to describe and interpret it. Where I have known that fleeting and deeply satisfying spiritual feeling of community, I have been caught up in it as a participant, not as an observer. My memory is that the feeling is closer to the religious and the social than to the artistic realm of experience. But certainly the artistic serial can weave in and out of such a context. That is, indeed, worthy of study, and I hope to do so, given grace and opportunity.

As to a formative hermeneutic relationship to community, I cannot easily conceive of it except as a parallel logical category. I can only conceive of a prophet, a saint, or a charismatic leader in such a connection, not of a person intent on knowing and appreciating.

Summary

This chapter has brought me close to a halt. It moves beyond my experience. I began writing it acknowledging that logic couldn't carry it through. I explored the idea of community and its very real meaning to me. I then projected a basis for group inquiry which I could comprehend from my present base of research into the making of art. This was a matter of shared worlds and influences between willing artists and observers. The emphasis remained on the individual artistic serial and on the compounding and transforming of information and influence related to this base.

In a search for examples, I referred to Smith's microethnography of the classroom and to the problems an advisee of mine has describing art student teachers by anthropological methods. Counelis' typology of generic research designs helped me to see how my emphasis differed from that of Smith and from most anthropologists (at least to a degree). The difference centered on the qualitative as opposed to the quantitative assumption about the time/space manifold, which focused me more on the contextual, unique historic event rather than on the case as exemplifying a generalized microcosm. Purity in such distinctions is not quite possible, it was concluded, but remains an operational goal. Under "Iconic Representations of the Group Setting," I tried to relate my conceptions to tangible summer class experiences I have had. Here the effort was to suggest the kinds of richness readily available for capturing group climate and action. Presentational, semi-expressive modes are easy extensions from this base.

Then historical modes in the group setting were discussed. Again, I tried to relate my thinking to my first experiences with group inquiry (with artists willing to share their recall of their art making). I was led to further reflections on the historical mode and its peculiar aptness for inquiry into the making of art (these reflections will be carried further in the next and final chapter).

In a further search for examples for methods, I referred in some detail to how the anthropologist Malinowski approached the complex task of describing a primitive culture. An anthropologist, it turns out, is part historian, part scientist, part philosopher (or so it seems to me). How he conducts himself gives us, in our present task, comfort and guidance.

Finally, I briefly explored, for conceptual symmetry, the idea of formative hermeneutic modes in the group setting. Such modes are practically beyond my present conceptual grasp, for reasons which I tried to disclose.

This chapter is acknowledged to be tentative. My own work has been closer to psychology and the individual history than to sociology or anthropology and the group history. But I recognize the logic that connects the one with the other, and see the opportunities for extending the one to the other. My deficiencies are experiential. I am just becoming ready to study the group history as it relates to the making of art. Apart from the scattered references I have reported, I have found very little guidance in the literature of art education to prepare me for this transition, either conceptually or methodologically.

7 Evaluation and Critique of Presentational, Phenomenological, and Contextualist Alternatives for Inquiry into the Making of Art

For all its unevenness and imperfection, I feel that (strangely for me) this is a coherent and unified book. I have not found it difficult to hold to the two major assumptions upon which it is based. What these sometimes lack in clarity and logic of presentation is counterbalanced by the feeling I consistently retain for them as guiding principles. Likewise, the ethic of the face-to-face, of the fullness of relationship to the artist, the acceptance of the idealized and internalized creative relationship which is the making of art, and my insistence that the study of these phenomena must contribute to their forward motion and potential in the world—these concepts have been richly sustained by my ongoing experience of inquiry. They do not seem like merely academic or logical issues.

My relationship, that is, to the very concepts and modes I present is itself creative and experiential. The limits of my powers stream from the same source. I prefer that such deficiencies as exist be taken as exemplifying some lack in my own sensitivities and desires, and not as intrinsic to the categories themselves. I know, for example, that chapters 5 and 6 are imperfectly represented, but since I can find no readier material, from myself or others, I present them for what they are, until the time better examples abound.

No mode is seen as finished. I have been brave or foolhardy enough to risk examples; of necessity these are imperfect and vulnerable. But if there is wisdom in the alternative routes proposed, even uneven examples may lead to faster correction and extension than taking refuge completely in abstract discussion. To make a comparison, while I am not prepared to speak authoritatively on phenomenology, I do know that those who can refer knowingly to its vast literature can scarcely point to examples of its method at work. I am, then, here raising the plea for patience and withholding of final judgment on the alternatives given, while nevertheless getting on with the task of evaluation and criticism.

Reflexivity in Art Education Research: Inquiry with a Conscience

For some reason, the self-correction and humility that are a common ingredient in our other actions—for example, in our teaching or our making of art—have been absent from our research. Traditionless and without masters in these activities, we have proceeded as though inflation and borrowing would dress us up. Before the making of art, we stand, epistemologically, like simpletons, but we are loathe to admit it. The degrees of insensitivity to the art making of others of which I and others have been guilty would bring us to legitimate despair were we not protected by ignorance, repression, and forgetfulness. The general stance and methods borrowed from psychology and educational research have helped to shade our eyes and minds from the obvious lack of touch we have with the phenomena central to our own field.

Such sweeping accusations are no less directed at myself than others. Nor do I accuse *any* methods in themselves as being faulty or the cause of our state of knowledge. In a sense, the way we have done our research has reflected the cultural climate in which art education is situated. Set within large group organizations, bureaucracies, and political forces, it has been hard for us to be reflexive. This is Gouldner's main point in his book, *The Coming Crisis in Western Sociology*.[1] We have not sufficiently admitted our own contamination and responsibility within the inquiry behavior itself, nor the effects of the myths rampant in an overdetermined scientific and technological cosmology. There is no fault to be found with so-called scientific, behavioral, or empirical methods as such, nor with computers, systems analysis, and the various managerial schemas of our large impersonal organizations. But a milieu which uncritically pushes only these, which is little concerned with correction and continuity, or which decides procedurally and within the spheres of institutional authority that *all* the facts worthy of study fall within their boundaries, is dogmatic and dangerous.

Reflexivity in inquiry calls for an acknowledgment of the fallibility, humanity, and, especially, the ongoing history of learning of the inquirers. To patience, humility and passion is added the virtue of ethical concern for the effects of inquiry itself. At bottom is not the politics of research, but a kind of awe and reverence for the phenomena themselves and an acknowledgment, as Collingwood puts it, that ". . . in the last resort nothing but the knower can be known."[2] The last ingredient returns us to philosophy itself and its necessary connection with all problems of inquiry and knowledge, regardless of method. It is this issue which brought us to contextualism as a viable world hypothesis and to a revised historical-psychological-philosophical base as our reasonable perspective on events.

This book does take sides, but it does so with no claim for completeness. My own wish is for pluralism in world view and in method. My perspective, as all perspectives, is partial. I have argued and will continue to argue for its justification and adequacy. But that is different from claiming for it what it cannot now or ever achieve, or for trying to thrust it dogmatically on everyone.

Further, even while I argue for pluralism, I must confess that inquiry itself leads one toward purity and exclusiveness. Any exclusiveness must nevertheless be positioned as one view within the many. Within the assumptions laid down herein and within the modes which I have presented, however, the reader will sense that I favor some over others.

What pervades this work is the desire to explore a range of modes not well represented in art education research. These modes have the clear virtue and difficulty of closeness to the unique, lived event. They opt for the concreteness of experience. They bring the issue of the knower of knowledge to the fore whereas traditional research conceals or removes it. If we go behind the modes of this book, and behind the assumptions I feel necessary to my inquiries, we arrive at the conclusion that Pepper did, that there are a number of world views which are undogmatic, autonomous, and cognitively adequate.[3] This is the pluralism for which I argue, even in working to correct existing imbalances and in pushing the strong conviction I feel for the methods I now use.

The Phenomenological and the Contextual-historical

I am not prepared to write with any confidence about phenomenology. As a method and as a philosophical position, there is a voluminous literature available to the interested reader. Mine, I suppose, is a layman's phenomenology, for it has some of the overtones that term takes on within American usage of the term "phenomenological psychology," where it pays homage to the knower's eye and world as these confront the world of another. It means the experiential, the qualitative account of phenomena, wherein knower and known are both essential parts of the equation of knowledge.

Stapleton, one of my present research assistants, is attempting to establish

> . . . the appropriateness of phenomenological description to the categories of contextualism. Both assume that knowledge and truth are accessible in present ongoing experiencing, the contents of which cannot be specified nor predicted except as outgrowths from the present. Contextualism stresses the intuition of the quality of wholeness which characterizes the present ongoing event; phenomenology stresses the intuited essence or structure which makes ongoing experiencing possible. Both came into being as first a methodology to describe empirically the structure of experiencing. Where phenomenology provides presentational descriptions of the structure of consciousness, the categories of contextualism provide a receptacle to retain and utilize phenomenological description. Both emphasize the relation of consciousness to the world as being man's intention. In short, I intend to make use of the mutual corroboration of the contextual categories to phenomenological description. The two taken together will be presented as a point of view which will provide a basis of describing a series of events consisting of a person coming into the drawing lab and my experience of that person's drawing.[4]

I have presented Stapleton's statement in some detail because it suggests an extension in sophistication beyond the level of my own arguments, on the one hand, and because it differently weights the contributions of phenomenology and contextualism to each other. The last sentence of the quotation also discloses the necessary relationship (one to be explored, not submerged) between another's making of art and the knower's experience of that occasion.

The matter of this relationship is complex. This book has centered upon it. I have taken the stand that a present, human relationship which explores the expressive act as lived history, shared by both artist and participant observer, is a sensitive path to knowledge (especially under the guise of appreciation and understanding) concerning creation. Dual first-person disclosures in the present are related, by stimulated recall, to joint exploration of the expressive situation in the past. The effort is to move as close to the creating stream of consciousness as possible, although this must be reflected through present intentions and consciousness. An infinite expansion occurs when the artistic serial takes on depth and when the private world of the artist and special participant observer merge, as they must, with the public, wider world context.

My own approach, perhaps a result of age, role, and temperament, is primarily nurturant and contextual. That is, I am passive, or receptive, to be as full as possible of the artist's action, feeling, and perception. I am less truly phenomenological than those better trained who follow me may be. My base is a simple reconstruction of a series of expressive situations, making use of the kinds of data my rituals of procedure produce. My reflections dwell upon the problem of the knowing mind, but I am capable of this only by stepping back, away from immersion in the artistic serial, gradually and slowly. From this point on, the contextual categories come into practical analytical play, as does my natural tendency to focus on the artist's evolving conscious cognitions about making art. I am also drawn to a hermeneutic or interpretive stance, but in this I am as an infant.

The Problem of Purity of World View and Method

Although I have spoken highly, and admiringly, of iconic and presentational modes, I gravitate most easily to a contextual-historical mode. Therein lies both strength and reason for despair. The effort at presentational modes seems doomed to failure when I take as my goal the concrete fact, unique and qualitative, and the knowing mind. An unavoidable self-consciousness arises. To escape this, I am attracted to the ideal of pure creation or expression. Sartre's hero in the novel, *Nausea*, Antoine Roquentin, has been trying to write a historical study of a French nobleman named Rollebon who lived in the latter eighteenth and early nineteenth century. Antoine has just turned up some new information, which he examines and speculates about. He then reflects on his interpretations:

> Well, yes: he could have done all that, but it is not proved. I am beginning to believe that nothing can ever be proved. These are honest hypotheses which take the facts into account: but I sense so definitely that they come from me, and that they are simply a way of unifying my own knowledge. Not a glimmer comes from Rollebon's side. Slow, lazy, sulky, the facts adapt themselves to the rigour of the order I wish to give them; but it remains outside of them. I have the feeling of doing a work of pure imagination. And I am certain that the characters in a novel would have a more genuine appearance, or, in any case, would be more agreeable.[5]

Here, then, is the one pole of despair that could lead one to a kind of purity. My own tendency is to lean in the other direction—away from "pure imagination." Yet tension with the presentational modes, as they are called in this book, is healthy. The most I can say, however, is that history (contextualism) is not art—it is a basic cognitive activity whose end is a kind of knowledge. But the direct statement, in art, of experience as though it is alive in all its qualitative richness and messiness does remain attractive; and, as Antoine says in the quote above, it appeals as something less arbitrary than taking some position, or forming some quite "honest hypotheses."

The Problems of Closeness and Distance

I do not fear, in this kind of inquiry, what some texts on anthropological method call "over-rapport." I believe this to be a fiction. As a human being intent on knowing another within the kind of context presented in this book, I cannot discern any line which means I am too close. I do have my natural preferences of relationship. I do not like to interrupt another person's art making, for example. I believe that closeness is really not a problem, except as it enters into the time rhythm which allows the person inquiring to step back gradually so that the details can fall back into a larger landscape.

Indeed, I would make the opposite case: one cannot grasp the condition of another's making art without closeness. In a recent article, Tsugawa raises an interesting parenthetical question in this regard:

> (can there be, of passional events, a nonparticipating agent who can be an objective observer and yet say anything worthwhile about the event?)[6]

The question's terms would need defining, but in the context of my present work, its knowledge goal, and its ethic, I would give a categorical "no" as an answer.

The nonparticipating agent who is an objective observer will not, I feel, say anything worthwhile about the reality of the expressive situation, about the experience of art, at least. I could hardly claim dogmatically that he could not make worthwhile observations. The question does arise as to what his position is, what his knowledge is for. Face to face with the live event, the person inquiring into the making of art can be neither the artist nor an utter stranger. Closeness and distance are tensional. They are built in by the role and the purpose of understanding and knowledge, without breaking thereby the human tie to the expressive situation; for, as we have just said, the tie between another's making of art and the knower's experience of that occasion is essential, unbreakable. The researcher's reflexivity, the phenomenology of his own experience of another's making art, are the cornerstones of a humanistic psychology of art.

My own vision of my entry into any given artistic serial is that of a friend or companion who shares and helps clarify the other through human interaction and concentration on his (the artist's) meaning and agency. Were speech not possible, or minimal, as with young children or those who cannot communicate for one reason or another, intentions and meanings would still be shared by whatever interpersonal means possible. Making art is not a purely private matter, though it proceeds from the lone center outward, and though the artist's agency and feeling are not directly accessible to another, no matter how close he be.

I discussed, in chapter 2, Jung's statement that "understanding" and "knowledge," as he used these terms, had to be kept in balance in the therapeutic setting. Such a balance occurs naturally in the rhythm of *inquiry from within the artistic serial.* By inclusion in the serial, art is a reality, for agency, meaning, intention, imagination, and the "otherness" of the expressive situation are all operative. The *artist's relation to himself* over time becomes a describable yet mythic affair, for the researcher is enclosed within a history of projection and transcendence. The historical-contextual analysis of projections and transcendences of an artistic serial (whose ultimate boundaries are the ends of a life), preferably studied by immersion within the ongoing serial, is the task I have set. The bounded context can be narrow or wide. The ingredients, I have assumed, are obtainable by way of indirect access to the creating stream of consciousness by way of a special, human, participant-observer role.

This task, that of a special kind of history, is of course idealized. It is, you may say, impossible. Granted, but the researcher attempting to operate under such modes cannot consign himself to utter skepticism or he will leave this special history altogether and work in philosophy proper. The same could be said for the scientist or the artist, both of whom proceed via a root metaphor imposssible but necesary to their operation.

I have here admitted to a kind of research that need not be called "scientific," although I do not feel "unscientific" either. The historical contextual stance centering on a qualitative grasp of the unique event, I have argued, is structurally closest to the humanistic tradition and lore of art, and to the way the expressive situation itself uniquely unfolds in time and space. I have no argument with the effort of "science" to subsume the individual, unique facts of expressive situations into particulars under some general perspective, except that, from the view of this book, such a procedure "degrades," as Collingwood puts it, history into science.[7] To degrade history to mere fact is precisely the task of science. But science presupposes history or contextualism and can never go beyond it.[8] Nor can the task of acquiring knowledge from the historical-contextual position be seen as subservient to the whims of art (whatever that means). The researcher who works under the modes called historical-contextual, steps within the art-making context to undergo, understand, and, eventually, describe, analyze, and interpret it. He will not worry that he cannot know the dancer from the dance (as Yeats put it). He will study the dancer and the dance simultaneously, utilizing all the responsive, empathic, interhuman, phenomenological means available to him. The passional, the projections and transcendences must touch the inquirer too. Hence, I said "over-rapport" is a funny term.

But what of distance? How is it achieved? How does one step backwards, humanly, reasonably—if not gracefully?

One of my present research assistants talks not of closeness and distance but of "stance" and "distance."[9] This clever distinction takes the oppositional character out of the terms and readily acknowledges the perspectivity and role character of both positions *vis à vis* the expressive situation. The special participant-observer stands as close as humanly possible to the expressive situation, imagining himself as within it. His receptive and responsive phases enter into the rhythm of an artistic serial constructed of cycles of making and reflecting, both concentrated on the artistic causality, idiosyncratic meaning, and intentional symbolism of the artist, as these are fleshed out in the stream of ongoing experience.

"Distance" is merely another stance—this time one of the special observer, and one, moreover, that becomes a changing ingredient in the knower's own inquiry serial. This change really constitutes learning as central to the knower's own history. It makes his reflexivity dynamic.

An example of this reflexivity is to be seen in Kenniston's Appendix A, "A Note on Research Involvement," to his book *Young Radicals*.[10] He confesses:

> . . . I myself became involved with those I was studying, found them an unusually likable group of young men and women, and was in sympathy with their over-all goals. I doubt that it is possible to study any human phenomenon without confronting the problem of the researcher's own involvement in his research and his research subject.[11]

He goes on to discuss the issue of personal involvement. Like Malinowski (in the citations of chap. 6 of this book), Kenniston has "foreshadowed problems" drawn from his training as a researcher and psychologist and, specifically, from his hypotheses about the psychological development of radicals. These hypotheses, it turns out, were in error, but it was essential to his inquiry to project them to find this out.

Other expectations he held were corrected by personal reactions. His interview methods did not threaten the young radicals, as he feared they would. And as he took a strong personal liking to them as individuals, he moved toward admiration and guilt, the latter occasioned by the omission from his own youth, in the early '50s, of any "Movement" and sense of commitment. Then comes the "distancing:"

> But perhaps the major change in my own involvement with the subjects of this book came simply as a result of trying to formulate generalizations sufficiently inclusive to describe most of them, yet sufficiently precise to give a sense of their distinctiveness. Rereading the transcripts of my interviews with these young radicals itself helped give me greater distance, just as the written record is more distant than the spoken word. And as I attempted to connect these young radicals with social forces and historical trends that affect us all, I gained greater perspective on what was indeed "special" about them, as on what seemed related in an important way to the post-modern world.[12]

Though my problem and Kenniston's are not identical, nevertheless the movement in and out of the phenomena of concern is similar. Indeed, everywhere I turn of late I find those concerned with the qualitative wholeness and complexity of human phenomena speaking in a similar vein. There are sufficient chapters on research involvement, theory, scope, and method, to form an anthology for solace and guidance for those of us willing to explore such alternatives as I try to present in this book.

Knower and Known

Despite the reflexivity which I insist is a necessary part of all inquiry, I may be seen by some readers to be traditional in my role differentiations. Immersion in the stream, the dialogue, the face-to-face, does not disguise the fact that such interactional phenomena still constitute an "object" of inquiry, although, admittedly, such usage of "object" is far from carrying its usual connotations of constancy and separation from the knower. I mean a broader usage of the terms. The expressive situation and the artistic serial are objects of inquiry in the way that a native village is for Malinowski, or the young radicals for Kenniston.

Some will also say that my two major assumptions are not only unnecessary but inept. Of these, a number will reject outright the qualitative presentational, historical-contextual, and formative hermeneutic modes as something less than, or other than, "science." Another, more radical, minority will feel that the artist can more profitably make himself and his artistic serial the object of his own inquiry, playing himself the alternating roles. What can be said of this latter claim?

It is only because the making, reflective cycles exist within art-life connections that the image of a coherent artistic serial constructed upon and constructive of a self-system arises. My feeling is that the inquirer can speak concerning this interactional system in another person, whereas the inquirer's study of his own, the knower's mind in time and space, in all its qualitative complexity, is more difficultly grasped, if indeed it can be analyzed at all by him, since it is part and parcel of the cybernetics of his own inquiry control system, an ongoing enterprise aided by reflexivity but never willingly totalized by it. The combined artist-inquirer suffers a similar fate. His reflexivity aids his serial; it does not apprehend or comprehend it.

The pragmatics of analysis and interpretation bring a working closure, a totality, to the study of expressive situations and artistic serials. Without claiming insight into the psychodynamics of the case, I would say one cannot do this well with oneself, anymore than he can close down on the artist when as inquirer, he has his stance within the artist's serial. At distance, he can do so. To a degree, I tried to do this to material from my own earlier life, in chapter 5, but I did not go much beyond using it to exemplify a concept under discussion.

With Buber, I believe that the self can have a living relationship only with otherness. But certainly the art dialogue itself is such an encounter. In that sense, the self can take as its object that encounter with otherness. In this issue, I draw no sharp lines, but argue pragmatically for the separation of roles.

Even with this separation we see cause enough for difficulty and no end to our task. Why should there be an end? What has ended or will end? I feel kinship with McCurdy as he tries to conceptualize the nature of personality:

> Personality is undoubtedly a multiplex unity. To try to come to final decisions, however, on the nature of the components which account for the multiplicity, and on the cause of the unity, is a supremely baffling task.[13]

The making of art is an equally or more baffling "multiplex unity." Very little can be held down or roped off if we are to study its potential range of meanings. What seem like facts, when taken as unique historic events are never just facts. We find, as Collingwood says, that every "concrete truth has an infinity of reasons (*rationes cognoscendi,* and for that matter *rationes essendi* as well)."[14]

Expansion of the Root Metaphor

Contextualism, with its open attention to the unique event, its unending but pragmatic analysis, provides the requisite shelter and dignity for our work. Further, it remains neutral as to contents, not closing down because of methodological dogma before inquiry ever begins. Into this neutrality, the lore and rich, qualitative complexity of art-making, and the equally "multiplex unity" of the self-system as represented in continuous artistic production, can enter in as contents. Phenomenological description and reflective introspection can join together in providing the richest possible basis for analysis according to contextualist categories. The stones that earlier builders rejected can indeed become the cornerstones of this new mental edifice. Titchener for example, in 1912 expressed his opinion that

> . . . . no form of phenomenology . . . can be truly scientific, for the reason that the implied attitude to experience is multiply motived and fluctuating, while the *minimum* requirement of science is a fixed and constant point of view.[15]

Indeed the attitude to experience we have been arguing is just what he says: multiply motived and fluctuating. From the qualitative side that is its very nature. Just as in a certain view of science one acts as though objectivity were possible, so in our view of inquiry we act as though a grasp of what is multiply motived and fluctuating were possible. The one moves by way of exclusion, the other by inclusion; one sets conceptual systems between knower and object, the other steps within the experiential stream. Neither, we hold, is in error. Both are part of the world of knowledge.

Twenty-four years after his book *World Hypotheses*, Pepper faced this potential conflict within the world of inquiry by showing that both conceptual and qualitative analysis belong within contextualism.[16] They complement one another, but they cannot be merged or reduced one to the other. He also revises the root metaphor for contextualism. In the earlier book, as we have indicated, it was the historic event; in the later one, it is the purposive act, or the appetitive structure. This shift is significant, for while purposive acts can be observed objectively, they assuredly conjure up the image of the human agent. All of this is implicit in the concept of the historic event, where there is a necessity to use action verbs—making, enjoying, solving, exploring, and the like; but direct reference to the purposive act makes this explicit.

Pepper shows that appetition (within which we can explore Levinas' distinction between desire as opposed to need[17]) can be analyzed in either a qualitative or conceptual manner. (By the latter he apparently means something akin to behavioristic social science, but this is not the place to get drawn into that debate.) It is Pepper's belief that both kinds of descriptions are true and necessary for full comprehension of our world:

> Though closely parallel, they are not exactly the same concepts. For the qualitative list does not automatically gear in with the conceptual system of the natural sciences, while the conceptual list does. It will be maintained that both of these lists are fully descriptive, in their own ways, of a purposive act. . . . We shall take each list seriously as a veridical description so far as observation has gone. If there have been errors, they are open to correction. A refinement of the concepts will always be possible. . . . At this point in the description of a purposive action, almost alone in the whole expanse of nature, we have both a highly articulated qualitative description and a highly articulated conceptual description which refer to exactly the same actual process. The bifurcation of nature into conceptual system, and qualitative experience meet here at this point. Here is where the crotch of the work is from which the bifurcation extends.
>
> My thesis will be that there is nothing wrong in this bifurcation. It was inevitable if our knowledge of the world was to increase. Once we understand it, and can trace it from its point of bifurcation to the tips of the prongs at the other end, we shall find it to be, not a source of division in our knowledge, but the very instrument for its comprehensive unification.[18]

I find this quotation a good one to summarize my own view. In order to disentangle myself from the uses and misuses of research in art education, I have had my own struggles with what Laing calls "the politics of experience."[19] I cannot fault science, conceptual description, or even the verificationist-objectivist stance. But I can deplore the misuse of these for purposes related to power and control.

> Positivism mystifies experience in that it requires one to experience things in the pseudo-scientific mode, objectivity. Personal events are experiential; to choose terms and syntax which objectify them is a political act that defines and distorts the human character of these events.[20]

Such a view is not overdrawn, given the texture of our social life. But in fairness, one cannot criticize conceptual description in and of itself—it is merely one of the prongs of the fork.

The making of art, however, is intensely personal and experiential. Hence I have begun, and literally only begun, to journey up the qualitative prong (I think of it visually as the left prong). What I have laid before the reader suffers from incompleteness, to be sure. It is a long way to the region of the tip of the prong (the tip itself I take to be unreachable).

The assumptions under which I have operated need not be those of other researchers interested in qualitative descriptions of the events and purposive acts comprising that multiplex unity, the expressive situation. I find them necessary to my present thought and action. The modes I have presented are not to be seen as techniques applicable in any direct fashion to any given context. As explorations in method they are barely a start. As techniques they cannot be applied like the logical operations within conceptual description (and even there techniques function poorly when they and not the ends of inquiry are the focus). My purpose was more to point out some of the features of this less known landscape for art education research.

I must hark back to the beginning of this book. If this effort of mine extensionalizes our knowledge and wonder before the making of art, its aim is well fulfilled. If it increases the quality of experience in the very artistic events it studies, or in those that follow it, its ethic is supportable. To claim anything more is inflated, to try anything less is to give up belief in art education and in the possibility of inquiry into the phenomena at its core.

Notes

Chapter 1

1. John Dewey, *Philosophy and Civilization* (New York: Minton, Balch and Co., 1931). See especially the chapters, "Qualitative Thought" and "Conduct and Experience."
2. John M. Anderson, *The Realm of Art* (University Park: Pennsylvania State University Press, 1967).
3. Noam Chomsky, *Language and Mind* (New York: Harcourt, Brace and World, 1968).
4. See Susanne K. Langer, *Philosophy in a New Key* (New York: Penguin Books, 1948). Also, Noam Chomsky, *Language and Mind*.
5. Viktor Lowenfeld, *Creative and Mental Growth*, 3rd ed. (New York: Macmillan Co., 1957).
6. Albert Dempsey, *A Descriptive Study in Ideational Patterns and the Evolution of Graphic Form in Drawings by Preschool Children* (unpublished doctoral dissertation, Pennsylvania State University, 1971).
7. Richard deCharms, *Personal Causation: The Internal Affective Determinants of Behavior* (New York: Academic Press, 1968).
8. Susanne K. Langer, *Mind: An Essay on Human Feeling* (Baltimore: The John Hopkins University Press, 1967).
9. Study conducted by Barbara White Kazanis, 1970, unpublished.
10. C. G. Jung, *Modern Man in Search of a Soul* (New York: Harcourt, Brace and Co., first published in 1933).
11. Herbert Read, *The Form of Things Unknown* (New York: Horizon Press, 1960).
12. Viktor Lowenfeld, *Creative and Mental Growth*.
13. Monroe C. Beardsley, review of Matthew Lipman's *What Happens in Art*, in *The Journal of Aesthetics and Art Criticism* 26 (Spring 1968):411-12.
14. Albert Dempsey, *A Descriptive Study*.
15. Rhoda Kellogg, *Analyzing Children's Art* (Palo Alto: National Press Books, 1969).
16. Susanne K. Langer, *Philosophy in a New Key*.
17. L. Wittgenstein, *Philosophical Investigations* (Oxford: Blackwell, 1963).
18. James Hogg, ed., *Psychology and the Visual Arts* (Middlesex: Penguin Books, 1969), p. 71.
19. C. G. Jung and C. Kerenyi, *Essays on a Science of Mythology* (Princeton: Princeton University Press, 1969).
20. Gordon W. Allport, "The Unique and the General in Psychological Science," *Journal of Personality*, (1962), 405-22.
21. Alvin W. Gouldner, *The Coming Crisis in Western Sociology* (New York: Basic Books, 1970). See especially "Toward a Reflexive Sociology," p. 488ff.
22. Stephen C. Pepper, *World Hypotheses* (Berkeley: University of California Press, 1942).
23. Susanne K. Langer, *Mind*.
24. P. W. Bridgman, *The Way Things Are* (Cambridge: Harvard University Press, 1966).
25. Kenneth R. Beittel, *Mind and Context in the Art of Drawing: An Empirical and Speculative Account of the Drawing Process and the Drawing Series and of the Contexts in Which They Occur* (New York: Holt, Rinehart, and Winston, 1972).
26. Dian Fetter, "Humanism [the New 'Catch-All?'] and the Ir-Rational World," *The Post House Review* 1 (July 1971): 34.

Chapter 2

1. Albert Tsugawa, "The Nature of the Aesthetic and Human Values," *Art Education* 21 (November 1968): 11-15, 20.

2. Dale B. Harris, *Children's Drawings as Measures of Intellectual Maturity* (New York: Harcourt, Brace and World, 1963).

3. Elliot Eisner, *A Comparison of the Developmental Drawing Characteristics of Culturally Advantaged and Culturally Disadvantaged Children* (Stanford: Stanford University, U.S.O.E. project no. 5-0237, ed 015 783, 1966).

4. Irvin L. Child, "Personal Preferences as an Expression of Aesthetic Sensitivity;" *Journal of Personality* 30 (1962):496-512, and "Aesthetic Judgment in Children," *Transaction* 7 (May 1970):47-51.

5. David Earl Burton, "Some Thoughts on an Aesthetic Education Curriculum" (unpublished term paper, Pennsylvania State University, March 1971).

6. R. G. Collingwood, *The Idea of History* (New York: Oxford University Press, 1946), p. 228.

7. Dale B. Harris, "Varieties of Observation." chap. 2, in Gordon Kensler, *Preconference Education Research Training Program for Descriptive Research in Art Education* (Washington, D.C.: National Art Education Association, U.S.O.E. project No. 0-0017, 1970), pp. 20-28.

8. Susanne K. Langer, *Mind: An Essay on Human Feeling* (Baltimore: The Johns Hopkins Press, 1967), p. 53.

9. Charles Sherman Steele, "A Theoretical Basis for Studying an Individual Making Art" (unpublished doctoral thesis, The Pennsylvania State University, 1971).

10. *Ibid*, p. 64.

11. R. G. Collingwood, *The Idea of History*, p. 314.

12. E. H. Gombrich, *Meditations on a Hobby Horse* (London: Phaidon, 1963), p. 51.

13. Alvin W. Gouldner, *The Coming Crisis of Western Sociology* (New York: Basic Books, 1970), p. 509.

14. Kenneth R. Beittel, *Effect of Self-reflective Training in Art on the Capacity for Creative Action* (University Park: The Pennsylvania State University, U.S.O.E., C.R.P. no. 1874, 1964), and *Selected Psychological Concepts as Applied to the Teaching of Drawing* (University Park: The Pennsylvania State University, U.S.O.E., C.R.P. no. 3149, 1966).

15. Catherine Patrick, "Creative Thought in Artists," *Journal of Psychology*, 4 (1937): 35-73.

16. Kenneth R. Beittel, *Mind and Context in the Art of Drawing* (New York: Holt, Rinehart and Winston, 1972).

17. Rudolf Arnheim, *Visual Thinking* (Berkeley: University of California Press, 1969), pp. 174-77.

18. Viktor Lowenfeld, *The Nature of Creative Activity* (New York: Harcourt Brace, 1939), and *Creative and Mental Growth*, 3rd ed. (New York: Macmillan Company, 1957).

19. Henry Schaefer-Simmern, *The Unfolding of Artistic Activity* (Berkeley, California: University of California, 1948).

20. Viktor E. Frankl, *The Will to Meaning* (New York: New American Library, 1969; Plune Book reprint, 1970), p. 152.

21. Ibid., pp. 23-25.

22. Erich Fromm, "On The Limitations and Dangers of Psychology," from *The Dogma of Christ* (New York: Holt, Rinehart and Winston, 1963), pp. 194, 195.

23. Ibid., p. 197.

24. Roger D. Barker, *Ecological Psychology* (Stanford: Stanford University Press, 1968).

25. Martin Buber, *Between Man and Man* (London: Kegan Paul, 1947), p. 179.

26. C. G. Jung, *The Undiscovered Self* (Boston: Little, Brown and Company, 1957; Mentor Book ed.), pp. 19-20.

27. Ibid., p. 62.

28. Ibid., pp. 63-64.

29. C. G. Jung, *Psychology and Alchemy* (New York: Pantheon Books, 1953).

30. Ibid., p. 45.

31. Ibid., pp. 43-44.

32. Louis M. Smith and William Geoffrey, *The Complexities of an Urban Classroom* (New York: Holt, Rinehart and Winston, 1968), and Louis M. Smith and Pat M. Keith, *Anatomy of Educational Innovation* (New York: John Wiley & Sons, 1971).

33. R. A. Barker and H. F. Wright, *Midwest and Its Children* (Evanston, Ill.: Row, Peterson, 1954), p. 199.

34. Albert Dempsey, "A Descriptive Study in Ideational Patterns and the Evolution of Graphic Form in Drawings by Preschool Children" (unpublished doctoral thesis, Pennsylvania State University, 1971).

35. Kenneth R. Beittel and Robert C. Burkhart, "Strategies of Spontaneous, Divergent, and Academic Art Sudents," *Studies in Art Education* 5 (Fall 1963):20-41.

36. Kenneth R. Beittel, *Effect of Self-reflective Training* and *Selected Psychological Concepts*.

37. Susanne K. Langer, *Mind*, pp. 272-273.

38. Louis M. Smith and J. A. M. Brock, *"Go, Bug, Go": Methodological Issues in Classroom Observational Research* (St. Ann, Missouri: Central Midwest Regional Educational Laboratory, Inc., 1970), pp. 8-11.

39. Paul Watzlawick, Janet Helmick Beaven, and Don D. Jackson, *Pragmatics of Human Communication* (New York: W. W. Norton, 1967), pp. 261-66.

40. P. W. Bridgman, *The Way Things Are* (Cambridge: Harvard University Press, 1966), p. 217.

41. Louis M. Smith, "Dilemmas in Educational Innovation: A Problem for Anthropology as Clinical Method" (unpublished paper presented at American Educational Research Association convention, Feb. 1971), p. 2.

42. Joseph Campbell, *The Masks of God: Creative Mythology* (New York: Viking Press, Compass ed. 1970), p. 673.

43. H. A. Murray and C. Kluckhohn, "Outline of a Conception of Personality," in C. Kluckhohn *et al., Personality in Nature, Society and Culture* (New York: Knopf, 1954), p. 12.

44. Ibid., p. 13.

45. Charles Sherman Steele, "A Theoretical Basis," p. 55.

46. Martin Buber, *Between Man and Man*, p. 31.

Chapter 3

1. Charles Sherman Steele, "A Theoretical Basis for Studying an Individual Making Art" (unpublished doctoral thesis, Pennsylvania State University, 1971).

2. Kenneth R. Beittel, *Effect of Self-Reflective Training in Art on the Capacity for Creative Action.* (University Park: Pennsylvania State University, U.S.O.E., C.R.P. no. 1874, 1964), and *Selected Psychological Concepts as Applied to the Teaching of Drawing* (University Park: Pennsylvania State University, U.S.O.E., C.R.P. no. 3149, 1966).

3. Roger D. Barker, *Ecological Psychology* (Stanford: Stanford University Press, 1968).

4. Charles Sherman Steele, "A Theoretical Basis," pp. 78-79.

5. Susanne K. Langer, *Mind: An Essay on Human Feeling* (Baltimore: The Johns Hopkins Press, 1967).

6. Charles Sherman Steele, "A Theoretical Basis," pp. 80-81.

7. Rudolf Arnheim, *Art and Visual Perception* (Berkeley: University of California, 1954).

8. Anton Ehrenzweig, *The Hidden Order of Art* (Berkeley: University of California Press, 1967).

9. Viktor Lowenfeld, *The Nature of Creative Activity* (New York: Harcourt, Brace, 1939).

10. Henry Schaefer-Simmer, *The Unfolding of Artistic Activity* (Berkeley: University of California Press, 1961).

11. Gustaf Britisch, *Theorie der Bildenden Kunst*, Egon Kornmann, ed. 2nd ed. Munich: Bruckman, 1930).

12. Kenneth R. Beittel, *Mind and Context in the Art of Drawing* (New York: Holt, Rinehart and Winston, 1972).

13. Ibid., see especially chap. 6 and 7.

14. Paul Watzlawick, Janet Helmick Beaven, and Don D. Jackson, *Pragmatics of Human Communication* (New York: W. W. Norton, 1967), pp. 261-66.

15. Ibid., p. 266.

16. Arthur Schopenhauer, *Die Welt als Wille und Vorstellung*, bk. 2, sect. 28 (vol. 2, pp. 202ff.) and bk. 4, sect. 55 (vol. 3, pp. 140ff.), in *Samtliche Werke* (Stuttgart: Cottasche Bibliothek der Weltlitteratur, no date).

Chapter 4

1. Emmanuel Levins, *Totality and Infinity* (Pittsburgh: Duquesne University Press, 1969), pp. 79-81.

2. Ibid., pp. 177-79.

3. William Butler Yeats, *The Autobiography of William Butler Yeats* (New York: Macmillan Co., 1938), p. 163.

4. Emmanuel Levinas, *Totality and Infinity*, pp. 72-77.

5. Ibid., pp. 116-17.

6. John Dewey, *Art as Experience* (New York: Minton, Balch & Co., 1934).

7. Jean Piaget, "Art Education and Child Psychology," in *Education and Art*, Edwin Ziegfeld, ed. (UNESCO, 1953), pp. 22-23.

8. Emmanual Levinas, *Totality and Infinity*, p. 300.

9. George C. Stern, "Measuring Noncognitive Variables in Research ou Teaching," chap. 9 in *Handbook of Research on Teaching*, N. L. Gage, ed. (Chicago: Rand McNally, 1963), p. 411.

10. Gordon W. Allport, *The Use of Personal Documents in Psychological Research* (New York: Social Science Research Council, 1942).

11. Kenneth R. Beittel, *Mind and Context in the Art of Drawing* (New York: Holt, Rinehart and Winston, Inc., 1972).

12. Gordon W. Allport, *The Use of Personal Documents*.

13. R. G. Collingwood, *The Idea of History* (New York: Oxford University Press, 1946). p. 314.

14. Eugene Gendlin, *Experiencing and the Creation of Meaning* (New York: Free Press, 1962).

15. Ibid., pp. 237-38.

16. Ibid., p. 28.

17. Caroline Georing Biss, "Influences Affecting the Nurturing of Artist-Craftsman Kenneth Beittel" (master's research paper in General Family Studies, Pennsylvania State University, College of Human Development, 1971).

18. Adrain van Kaam, *Existential Foundations of Psychology* (Garden City, N.Y.: Image Books, 1969), pp. 15-23. (A paperback of the original Duquesne Universities Press edition, 1966.)

19. Stephen C. Pepper, *World Hypotheses* (Berkeley: University of California Press, 1970; original copyright, 1942).

20. Ibid., p. 232.

21. Ibid., . 233.

23. Ibid., pp. 233-34.

23. Ibid., pp. 235-36.

24. Ibid., pp. 237-38.

25. Ibid., pp. 238-39.

26. Ibid., p. 260.

27. Ibid., p. 261.

28. Ibid., p. 256.

29. Ibid., pp. 262-63.

30. Jean Piaget, *Structuralism* (New York: Basic Books, 1970), p. 14.

31. Ibid., pp. 52-53.

32. Ibid., p. 53.

33. Ibid., p. 53.

34. Stephen C. Pepper, *World Hypotheses*, p. 264.

35. Ibid., p. 264.

36. Ibid., p. 265.

37. Rudolf Arnheim, *Visual Thinking* (Berkeley: University of California Press, 1969), pp. 174-77.

38. Viktor Lowenfeld, *The Nature of Creative Activity* (New York: Harcourt Brace, 1939), and *Creative and Mental Growth*, 3rd ed. (New York: Macmillan Co., 1957).

39. Henry Schaeffer-Simmern, *The Unfolding of Artistic Activity* (Berkeley: University of California, 1948).

40. Rudolf Arnheim, "Child Art and Visual Thinking," pp. 44-45 in Lewis, Hilda Present, ed., *Child Art: The Beginning of Self-Affirmation* (Berkeley, California: Diablo Press, 1966).

41. Clark E. Moustakas, *Psychotherapy with Children* (New York: Ballatine Books, 1970; original copyright, 1959).

42. Robert Coles, *Children of Crisis* (New York: Dell Publishing Co., a Delta Book, 1967).

43. Ibid., pp. 40-41.

44. Ibid., p. 44.

45. Stephen C. Pepper, *World Hypotheses*, p. 148.

46. Ibid., p. 146.

47. *Webster's New International Dictionary of the English Language,* 2nd ed., unabridged (Springfield, Mass.: G & C Merriam Co., Publishers, 1959), p. 1168.

48. Morris Philipson, *Outline of a Jungian Aesthetics* (Champaign, Ill.: Northwestern University Press, 1963), p. 66.

49. Ibid., p. 65.

50. Ibid., p. 62.

Chapter 5

1. André Malraux, *The Voices of Silence* (New York: Doubleday & Co., 1953).

2. Marion Milner, *On Not Being Able to Paint* (New York: International Universities Press, Inc., 1957).

3. Robert Jay Lifton, *Boundaries: Psychological Man in Revolution* (New York: Vintage Books, 1970).

4. Ibid., pp. 105-6.

Chapter 6

1. Emmanuel Levinas, *Totality and Infinity* (Pittsburgh: Duquesne University Press, 1969).

2. Martin Buber, *Between Man and Man* (London: Kegan Paul, 1947).

3. Alvin W. Gouldner, *The Coming Crisis in Western Sociology* (New York: Basic Books, 1970).

4. Kenneth Burke, *Attitudes Toward History* (Boston: Beacon Press, 1961; paperback issue of 1937, 1959 ed., p. 234.

5. Louis M. Smith and William Geoffrey, *The Complexities of an Urban Classroom* (New York: Holt, Rinehart and Winston, 1968), and Louis M. Smith and Pat M. Keith, *Anatomy of Educational Innovation* (New York: John Wiley and Sons, 1971).

6. Louis M. Smith, "Vignettes on Package Utilization," X pilot memo #16, April 3, 1972, pp. 1-2 (St. Ann, Missouri: CEMREL, Inc.).

7. Ibid., p. 10.

8. James Steve Counelis, "A Typology of Generic Research Designs," *Division Generator* 2 (March 1972); 9-12.

9. Ibid., p. 10.

10. Ibid.

11. Ibid., pp. 10-11.

12. Louis M. Smith and William Geoffrey, *The Complexities of an Urban Classroom.*

13. Stephen C. Pepper, *World Hypotheses* (Berkeley: University of California Press, 1970; original copyright, 1942).

14. Kenneth R. Beittel, *Mind and Context in the Art of Drawing* (New York: Holt, Rinehart and Winston, 1972).

15. Bronislaw Malinowski, *Argonants of the Western Pacific* (London: George Routledge and Sons, 1932).

16. Ibid., p. 9.

17. Ibid., p. 11

18. Ibid.

19. Ibid., p. 12-13.

20. Ibid., p. 25.

Chapter 7

1. Alvin W. Gouldner, *The Coming Crisis in Western Sociology* (New York: Basic Books, 1970).

2. R. G. Collingwood, *Speculum Mentis* (Oxford: Clarendon Press, 1924), p. 245.

3. Stephen C. Pepper, *World Hypotheses* (Berkeley: University of California Press, 1970; original copyright, 1942).

4. Don J. Stapleton, "Metaphysical Assumptions and Methodological Extensions of a Contextual View of Research in Art Education" (unpublished research proposal, Department of Art Education, Pennsylvania State University, May 18, 1972), pp. 10-11.

5. Jean-Paul Sartre, *Nausea* (New York: New Directions paperback, 1959), p. 23.

6. Albert Tsugawa, "Art, Knowledge and Love," *Art Education* 25 (May 1972), p. 7.

7. R. G. Collingwood, *Speculum Mentis,* p. 208.

8. Ibid., p. 202.

9. Don J. Stapleton, The concepts referred to came out in a discussion with the author.

10. Kenneth Kennison, *Young Radicals* (New York: Harcourt, Brace and World, 1968), pp.291-96.

11. Ibid., p. 291.

12. Ibid., p. 295.

13. Harold Grier McCurdy, *The Personality of Shakespeare* (New Haven: Yale University Press, 1953), p. 37.

14. R. G. Collingwood, *Speculum Mentis,* p. 245.

15. E. B. Titchener, "The Schema of Introspection," *Journal of Psychology* 23 (Oct. 1912): 490.

16. Stephen C. Pepper, *Concept and Quality* (LaSalle, Ill.: Open Court Publishing Co., 1966).

17. Emmanual Levinas, *Totality and Infinity* (Pittsburgh: Duquesne University Press, 1969).

18. Stephen C. Pepper *Concept and Quality,* pp. 26-27.

19. R. D. Laing, *The Politics of Experience* (New York: Ballantine, 1967).

20. T. R. Young, *New Sources of Self* (New York: Pergamon Press, 1972).

Index